SCANDALOUS!

First published in 2012 by Zest Books
35 Stillman Street, Suite 121, San Francisco, CA 9410
www.zestbooks.net
Created and produced by Zest Books, San Francisco, CA

Typeset in Sabon and Trade Gothic
Teen Nonfiction / History / People & Places United States

Library of Congress Control Number: 2011936079

ISBN: 978-0-9827322-0-5

CREDITS
EDITORIAL DIRECTOR: Karen Macklin
BOOK EDITORS: Karen Macklin and Maria Wakem
CREATIVE DIRECTOR: Hallie Warshaw
ART DIRECTOR/COVER DESIGN: Tanya Napier
PRODUCTION ARTIST: Marissa Feind
MANAGING EDITOR/PRODUCTION EDITOR: Pam McElroy
RESEARCH AND MARKETING DIRECTOR: Nikki Roddy

TEEN ADVISORS: Amelia Alvarez, Ema Barnes, Anna Livia Chen, Huitzi Herrera-Sobal, and Felicity Massa

Manufactured in China
LEO 10 9 8 7 6 5 4 3 2 1
4500325577

All photos courtesy of the Everett Collection with the exception of pages 123, 131, 151, 167, and 203, which are courtesy of Getty Images; pages 75 and 83, which are courtesy of Photofest; and page 107, which is courtesy of The National Archives.

SCANDALOUS!

50 SHOCKING EVENTS YOU SHOULD KNOW ABOUT (SO YOU CAN IMPRESS YOUR FRIENDS)

by Hallie Fryd

INTRODUCTION

➡ **Everyone loves a good scandal.** Why? Because scandals are exciting, juicy stories with lots of twists and turns. They involve dramatic trials and fallen celebrities, misguided scientists and game-changing athletes, superstar lawyers, hardened criminals, and all kinds of secrets and lies. Plus, they make great conversation at parties. But when you really break it down, scandals are also an important part of history. Something is considered "scandalous" because it's wrong or immoral in our eyes. The things we find shocking can tell us a lot about ourselves and our society.

Scandals are cornerstones, too, in a society's evolution. For instance, Elvis' scandalous hip-shaking on TV set the stage for rock stars to use sex-appeal in performances. The Jonestown Massacre made people wary of cult religions that cut members off from society. The Clarence Thomas scandal made Americans more aware of sexual harassment. And the Scopes Monkey Trial changed the way science is taught in classrooms across the country.

From Hollywood murder trials to spies, anarchists, money-grubbing televangelists, explicitly sexual art, vigilante justice, and Harvard psychedelic studies, the 50 scandals in this book span the 20th century and have all affected the trajectory of our country in some way. They touch on every part of society: politics, music, religion, sports, war, race relations, art, TV, movies, journalism, gay rights, and everything in between. Each item in *Scandalous!* details what happened in the scandal, offers unbelievable quotes, talks about how the event affected American culture and politics, and includes a short list of related scandals (so you can see how, sometimes, history is doomed to repeat itself!).

After you read *Scandalous!*, you'll have a better understanding of how things in all realms of life have gotten to be the way they are today. And you may even become a history buff while you're at it.

—Hallie Fryd

TABLE OF CONTENTS

TABLE OF CONTENTS

THE SCOOP!

A famous architect is murdered by the millionaire husband of an ex-lover resulting in one of the first highly publicized trials of the 20th century.

WHAT WENT DOWN

Stanford White, a 47-year-old married architect, was famous for building houses for America's richest families and for throwing intimate parties at his secret pad, where he entertained pretty teenage chorus girls and models. His favorite pastime was pushing them, in various states of undress, on a red velvet swing he had installed in his apartment. One of those girls was Evelyn Nesbit, a 16-year-old model and Broadway chorus girl famous for being one of the most beautiful women in New York City. After a few rides on White's swing, Nesbit lost her virginity to him and spent the next two years as his mistress.

When White lost interest in her, Nesbit started spending time with Harry Thaw, the 31-year-old wealthy son of a Pittsburgh railroad tycoon. Thaw proposed to Nesbit shortly after they met, but he was no Prince Charming. He was a hard partier, wildly jealous, and once beat Nesbit brutally with a whip. But she married him anyway in 1905 and moved with him to his hometown of Pittsburgh.

During a visit to the Big Apple a year later, the couple went to see a musical comedy on the roof of Madison Square Garden, a building designed by White, who was also at the show. Near the end of the performance, Thaw walked down the aisle toward White,

THE PLAYERS

➡ Evelyn Nesbit
Model and Chorus Girl

➡ Stanford White
Murdered Architect

➡ Harry Thaw
Millionaire Murderer

took out a gun, and shot White three times in the head. The architect slumped to the ground dead, and Thaw walked calmly to the elevator where he was stopped and taken into custody.

The trials that followed were a sensation from the start. Everyone involved was rich and famous, and the press delighted in digging up the dirtiest details of White's private life (like his red velvet swing). Thaw hired the best defense lawyers who used the public's growing disgust of White in their favor. They argued that Thaw had gone temporarily insane when he saw White at the show, remembering White's past creepy involvement with his young wife.

Harry Thaw in 1906, awaiting trial in a posh prison.

QUOTEABLES

"He ruined my wife." (Or, "He ruined my life.")

Witnesses disagree about which one of these statements Harry Thaw made while being taken into custody by police following Stanford White's murder.

"What was his condition of mind when he first beheld White? He stood there beholding the figure, the hideous figure of the man that caused him so much sorrow... He struck as does the tigress strike at the man who endeavors to take her cubs. He struck for the purity of the wives and homes of America."

Part of the closing arguments made by one of Thaw's lawyers in his first trial.

Behind the scenes, Thaw's mother used the family fortune to further defend her son. She funded a biased film that portrayed Thaw as a hero who was simply defending his wife's honor, an act many people in America supported. Thaw's mother also offered Nesbit a quick divorce and a million dollars to stand by Thaw. (The public didn't know about the bribe.) At the trial, Nesbit testified that White had raped her when she was a 16-year-old virgin, and that she had told Thaw about it before they married, which planted a seed of madness in his mind. After her testimony, Thaw was seen as a hero who had avenged his wife's honor against a cruel pervert. In 1908, after two trials, Thaw was declared not guilty by reason of insanity and was sentenced to serve time in a low-security asylum in Upstate New York.

THE AFTERMATH

Harry Thaw: Thaw's hero status and wealth allowed him to live comfortably in the asylum. He escaped to Canada in 1913 but was eventually extradited, forced to return to the US, and put in the assylum. In 1915, he was declared sane and released. But just one year later, he was sentenced to another seven years in an asylum after sexually assaulting and brutally horsewhipping a teenage boy.

Evelyn Nesbit: Nesbit got her divorce in 1916, but not her million dollars. She also gave birth to a son who she said was Thaw's, but Thaw refused to claim him. Without financial support, Nesbit was forced to return to acting where she had little success. She struggled with suicide attempts in the 1920s, and then lived a quiet life teaching ceramics and sculpting. Before she passed away at 82, she published two memoirs: *The Story of My Life* in 1914 and *Prodigal Days* in 1934. Joan Collins played Evelyn Nesbit in a 1955 film inspired by the trial, *The Girl in the Velvet Swing*. Nesbit, Thaw, and White also inspired the novel/musical/movie *Ragtime*.

WHY WE STILL CARE

⭐ **Harry Thaw proved that with the right publicity, a criminal can get off easy.** Thaw shot a man in the face in front of a crowd of witnesses. But with the help of the press, his expensive lawyers, and his mother, the public viewed him as a gentleman defending his wife's honor against a pervert. Instead of the death penalty, which was the usual punishment for murderers at the time, he was sentenced to just a few years in a minimum-security asylum.

⭐ **The case was one of the first highly publicized trials of the century.** It came at a time when new paper and production technology was drastically cutting the cost of producing a newspaper. The new technology meant lots of new newspapers on the scene, and the story about Stanford White's murder made headlines and drove sales in all of them.

MORE CRIMES OF PASSION

➡️ **John Hinckley, Jr.** When Hinckley saw actress Jodie Foster in the movie *Taxi Driver*, it was love at first sight. The 25-year-old love-struck fan figured that the best way to get Foster's attention was through some sort of grand gesture, like shooting the president. So in March of 1981, he waited with a gun outside the Washington Hilton for President Reagan to come out. He fired six times, wounding the President and three others. At the trial, his defense lawyers used Hinckley, Jr.'s obsession with Foster to prove he was crazy. He was found not guilty by reason of insanity and was sent to a mental hospital in Washington, DC.

➡️ **Amy Fisher.** Mary Jo Buttafuoco should never have opened her front door in May of 1992. On the other side was her husband's 17-year-old mistress, Fisher, who barely hesitated before shooting Mrs. Buttafuoco in the face. Mary Jo (amazingly) survived and Fisher (who the media dubbed the Long Island Lolita) was found guilty of attempted murder and sentenced to up to 15 years in jail.

➡️ **Lisa Nowak.** Astronaut Nowak had a crush on fellow astronaut William Oefelein, so she drove 900 miles to confront Colleen Shipman, a woman she considered a rival for Oefelein's love. Nowak sprayed pepper spray into Shipman's car (the window was rolled down), but Shipman managed to get away. Nowak was later kicked out of NASA and sentenced to community service and anger management classes after pleading guilty to car burglary and assault.

WRITER UPTON SINCLAIR EXPOSES MEAT INDUSTRY'S NASTY UNDERBELLY

1906

THE SCOOP!

Meat production in the early 1900s was a dangerous and disgusting job, but most Americans stayed blissfully in the dark about how their sausage was made. That is, until Upton Sinclair's novel *The Jungle* exposed the meat industry for what it was.

THE PLAYERS

➡️ Upton Sinclair
Acclaimed Author

➡️ Chicago Meatpackers
Dirty-Job Workers

WHAT WENT DOWN

The Industrial Revolution in the 18th and 19th centuries led to major changes in the way almost everything was produced, from hamburgers to cars. Machines and human assembly lines were rapidly replacing family farms and skilled artisans. But while technology definitely helped speed things up, it also caused a new set of problems, especially for the workers manning the machines.

In 1904, struggling writer Upton Sinclair was offered $500 by a socialist newspaper, *Appeal to Reason*, to write an article about wage slaves (i.e., workers whose livelihoods are completely dependent on the little money they are earning at their jobs). He traveled to Chicago's Packingtown neighborhood, an area known for its slaughter houses and meatpacking plants. Sinclair spent seven weeks in Packingtown touring these places and talking with workers about the dangerous and unsanitary conditions they had to deal with on the job.

Sinclair used the information he uncovered to write a novel called *The Jungle*, which *Appeal to Reason* published as an ongoing series. *The Jungle* revolved around the Rudkus family, a fictional immigrant family who all worked as meatpackers in Chicago. Sinclair created the

A 1906 poster advertising The Jungle.

characters to show how poorly these workers were treated and how unsanitary and unsafe it was for them in the slaughterhouses and canning plants. The book was full of disgusting details of diseased cattle being canned for the public to eat, men sticking their unwashed hands into vats of meat, and poisoned rats getting mixed up with meat that was then turned into sausages. Sinclair even wrote about how workers sometimes fell into vats of boiling lard and weren't fished out until all that was left were some random bones. But readers of *The Jungle* seemed less worried about meatpackers losing their thumbs at work and more worried about all those missing thumbs ending up in their breakfast sausages.

The novel became an instant success and was translated into 17 languages, while sales of American meat fell by half almost immediately after the story

QUOTEABLES

"I aimed at the public's heart, and by accident I hit it in the stomach."

Upton Sinclair's famous reaction to the success of *The Jungle*.

"[The] rats were nuisances, and the packers would put poisoned bread out for them; they would die, and then rats, bread, and meat would go into the hoppers together."

An excerpt from *The Jungle* on the disgusting conditions at the meatpacking plant.

came out. Under public pressure, President Teddy Roosevelt sent government officials to investigate the meatpacking industry to find out if Sinclair was telling the truth or just exaggerating to sell books. The officials agreed with Sinclair: The meatpacking industry was disgusting and needed to be reformed. Less than six months later, Congress passed the Meat Inspection Act and the Pure Food and Drug Act of 1906, both of which led to the development of the Food and Drug Administration (FDA), which we still depend on today to make sure our food is safe.

☆ **Upton Sinclair inspired generations of investigative journalists.** He was part of a group of early-20th-century writers called "muckrakers," who, in order to promote social change, wrote stories to show the public what was wrong and unfair with the newly industrialized world. This brand of hardcore journalism is what inspired the high investigative journalism standards of today.

THE AFTERMATH

Upton Sinclair: By the time Sinclair died at age 90 in 1968, he had written almost 100 works of fiction and nonfiction. He won the Pulitzer Prize in 1943 for his novel *Dragon Teeth*, and his 1927 novel *Oil!* was made into the 2007 movie *There Will be Blood*, which was nominated for eight Academy Awards and won two Oscars.

The Meatpackers: In the 1920s, meatpackers started to form unions, which allowed them to demand better working conditions and higher pay for their work. From the 1930s to the 1980s, meatpackers actually made a little more than other manufacturing workers. But in the late 1980s, manufacturing centers started moving out of cities and into rural areas and were mostly staffed by illegal immigrants who were afraid to unionize. Since then, pay has gone steadily down and conditions have, unfortunately, gotten worse again.

☆ *The Jungle* **began a long line of investigations into where our food comes from.** When industrialization changed the way America's meat was produced, no one really paid attention. But after people read the stomach-turning revelations in *The Jungle*, the government was forced to create the Food and Drug Administration. Since then, there have been many mainstream investigations into what we are eating, including movies like *Food, Inc.* and *Earthlings*, investigative stories about mad cow disease and salmonella, and campaigns by animal rights organizations like PETA.

MORE FOOD CONTAMINATION HORROR STORIES

➡ **Listeria Bacteria.** In early 1985, 86 people living in and around Los Angeles got sick from eating soft Mexican cheese contaminated with listeria bacteria, resulting in 40 deaths. Since listeria usually infects unpasteurized dairy products, both the owner of the company that made the cheese and the guy in charge of pasteurization served jail sentences.

➡ **E. Coli.** The fast-food chain Jack in the Box was serving burgers with a side of flesh-eating e. coli bacteria in Washington State in 1993. Three children died and more than 500 people were affected, 144 of whom had to be hospitalized. Investigators blamed meat inspection techniques, which hadn't changed since 1906 and mainly involved looking at, and sniffing, meat to see if it seemed okay.

➡ **Melamine.** Back in 2007, the FDA had to recall 60 million cans of pet food that had been sent to the US from China because the food was tainted with melamine, a chemical used to make plastic. The contaminated food killed 14 pets. But that's only half the story. A year later, melamine was found in baby formula produced by Chinese baby-food manufacturers. The formula never made it to the US but was sold in China, killing one Chinese baby and giving 50 more kidney damage.

➡ **Salmonella.** In 2008, more than 500 people got sick and 8 died from eating peanuts from the Peanut Corporation of America that were tainted with salmonella. When the FDA investigated the plants where the peanuts were processed, they found lots of mold, rodents, and insects. They also discovered that the company had knowingly shipped the contaminated products. Unfortunately for the victims, the company declared bankruptcy after getting caught, so there was no one to sue.

THE SCOOP!

Native American athlete Jim Thorpe's record-breaking performance at the 1912 Summer Olympics in Stockholm earned him two gold medals. But six months later, Thorpe was forced to return his medals for reasons that many felt were unjust and racist.

WHAT WENT DOWN

Jim Thorpe was born in 1888. He grew up poor, but showed great promise as a teenage athlete. At Carlisle Indian School in Pennsylvania, he became an all-star football player while competing in 10 other sports and even winning an inter-collegiate ballroom dancing competition. Thanks to his unbelievable athletic ability, Thorpe easily made the US track and field team and was then chosen to compete in the 1912 Summer Olympics in Stockholm, Sweden. There, he competed in the pentathlon (which combines 5 different track-and-field events) and the decathlon (which combines 10 track-and-field events). No single athlete had ever won the pentathlon and decathlon in the same Olympic games, but Thorpe creamed the competition with record-breaking scores and won gold medals in both events. He returned to the US a national hero and even got his own ticker-tape parade in New York City.

The glory didn't last long, though. That fall, a reporter named Roy Johnson dug up information that showed Thorpe hadn't technically been an "amateur athlete" during the

THE PLAYERS

➜ Jim Thorpe
The Native American Athlete

➜ Roy Johnson
A Troublemaking reporter

➜ Amateur Athletic Union
Gold Medal Retractors

Olympics. He had made up to $35 per week playing minor league baseball in North Carolina during the summers of 1909 and 1910. Today, professional athletes (i.e., anyone who earns money playing sports) are allowed to compete in the Olympics, but back then it was against the rules. Still, a lot of college athletes played for extra cash at the time. They just knew to use a fake name to protect their amateur status. Unfortunately, Thorpe—who, as a Native American, and an outsider to mainstream sports—didn't know about this trick. He had used his real name when he played for pay, making it easy to prove that he violated the rules.

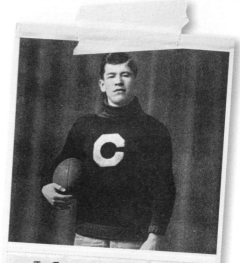

Jim Thorpe as a young football star at Carlisle Indian Institute.

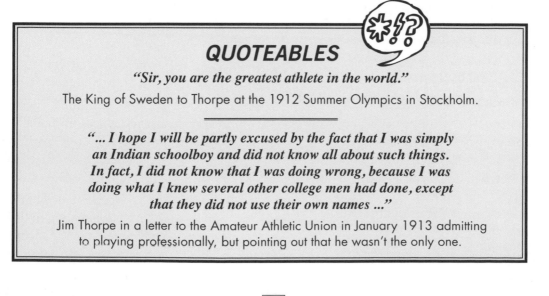

QUOTEABLES

"Sir, you are the greatest athlete in the world."

The King of Sweden to Thorpe at the 1912 Summer Olympics in Stockholm.

"... I hope I will be partly excused by the fact that I was simply an Indian schoolboy and did not know all about such things. In fact, I did not know that I was doing wrong, because I was doing what I knew several other college men had done, except that they did not use their own names ..."

Jim Thorpe in a letter to the Amateur Athletic Union in January 1913 admitting to playing professionally, but pointing out that he wasn't the only one.

Six months after the 1912 Summer Olympics, Johnson published an article in *The Worchester Telegram* with his findings about Thorpe. Although Thorpe was technically guilty, the allegations in the article shouldn't have done anything to his Olympic status. According to official Olympic rules, if you want to challenge an athlete's qualifications you need to do it within 30 days of the games. But, the Amateur Athletic Union (AAU) demanded a response from Thorpe about the allegations. Thorpe admitted to having played ball in college for money, and so the AAU insisted that he return his gold medals to the International Olympic Committee (IOC), and stripped Thorpe of his two big wins.

WHY WE STILL CARE

☆ **The scandal is seen as a symbol of injustice.** The Olympic rule regarding challenging an athlete's qualifications was clear. So Thorpe should have never been stripped of his medals. While it is difficult to prove, many sports historians believe that the only reason Thorpe was disqualified was because of the prevalent racism against Native Americans at the time.

THE AFTERMATH

Jim Thorpe: Thorpe went on to play six years of pro baseball for the New York Giants, Cincinnati Reds, and Boston Braves, where he was a fan favorite. He also played and coached pro football (at the same time) and helped form the National Football League (NFL), eventually becoming the first league president. In 1953, Thorpe suffered a heart attack while eating dinner and died at 64. In 1982, the IOC reinstated Thorpe's gold medals and gave replicas of them to two of his kids. In an Associated Press poll of sports writers and sports broadcasters, Thorpe was ranked the best athlete of the first half of the 20th century. He has since been inducted into the College Football Hall of Fame, the Pro Football Hall of Fame, and the US Olympic Team Hall of Fame.

☆ **The scandal called attention to the unfair rules of amateurism.** When the modern Olympics began in 1896, one of the first rules imposed was that all competing athletes had to be amateurs, meaning they couldn't make even $1 playing sports. Working-class Americans saw the rule as unfair because it favored wealthy athletes who didn't need to earn money to support themselves while training in their chosen sport. However, it wasn't until the 1970s that Olympic rules on amateurism started to loosen up. Now almost every Olympic sport allows pros to compete.

MORE OLYMPIC ATHLETES WHO BROKE THE RULES

➡ ***Eleanor Holm.*** This Olympic swimmer was caught drinking champagne (gasp!) on the boat that carried the American team to the 1936 Olympics in Berlin. She had received a warning already from Olympic officials for drinking alcohol and breaking curfew, which were against Olympic rules. So as soon as the boat hit the shore, Holm was dropped from the team.

➡ ***Barbara Ann Scott.*** This Canadian figure skater was forced to give back a new yellow convertible that Canadian fans gave her after winning both the European and World Skating Championships in 1947 on the grounds that any payment—even gifts—would make her a pro and therefore ineligible to compete in the 1948 Olympics.

➡ ***Ara Abrahamian.*** This Swedish Greco-Roman wrestler won a bronze medal in the 2008 Olympics, but he thought he deserved better. So right in the middle of the medal ceremony he took off his bronze medal, dropped it on the ground, and stormed out of the room. According to the International Olympic Committee (IOC), Abrahamian's angry outburst violated the spirit of fair play. He was stripped of his medal and his athletic credentials.

THE SCOOP!

In an attempt to remove gay men from the Navy, officers Ervin Arnold and Erastus Hudson created an undercover scheme that wound up scandalizing the nation and putting the Navy on trial before Congress.

WHAT WENT DOWN

Ervin Arnold was a conservative Navy officer stationed at the Newport Naval Training Station in Rhode Island at the end of World War I. After spending some time in Newport, he didn't like what he saw: There was a thriving gay community in Newport, and some of the sailors had become a part of it, partying with—and messing around with—other men. Some of these sailors even openly referred to themselves as the "Ladies of Newport." Back then, sexual acts between two men were against the law and homosexuals were scorned by society. The idea that there were openly gay men in the Navy did not sit well with Arnold.

Arnold teamed up with Erastus Hudson—an equally conservative Navy lieutenant—and hatched a plan to bust the gay sailors. They went to the Assistant Secretary of the Navy, Franklin Roosevelt (who would become president more than a decade later), with a plan to root out the gay sailors, and Roosevelt gave them the go-ahead.

Arnold and Hudson recruited a team of undercover "operatives"—young (sometimes teenage) Navy men who were sent

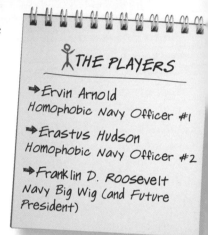

THE PLAYERS

➡ Ervin Arnold
Homophobic Navy Officer #1

➡ Erastus Hudson
Homophobic Navy Officer #2

➡ Franklin D. Roosevelt
Navy Big Wig (and Future President)

out to party with and seduce fellow saiors, then write up reports detailing their sexual exploits with the gay sailors. They were given immunity for breaking gay sex laws since they were on a military mission. Seventeen gay sailors were caught in the sting, and some of them ended up in jail. If Arnold and Hudson had stopped there, they might have kept their unethical plan under wraps. But they decided their operation would be great for catching all the gays in all of Newport, and Roosevelt gave them the permission and the funds they needed to do it.

Young Navy officers hanging out in the early 1900s.

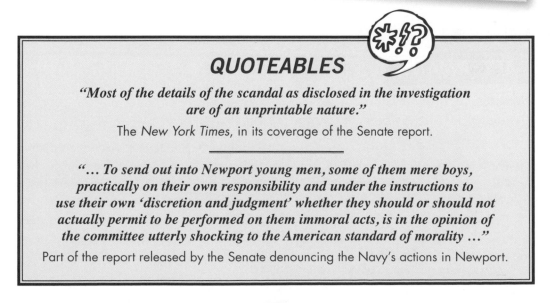

QUOTEABLES

"Most of the details of the scandal as disclosed in the investigation are of an unprintable nature."

The *New York Times*, in its coverage of the Senate report.

"… To send out into Newport young men, some of them mere boys, practically on their own responsibility and under the instructions to use their own 'discretion and judgment' whether they should or should not actually permit to be performed on them immoral acts, is in the opinion of the committee utterly shocking to the American standard of morality …"

Part of the report released by the Senate denouncing the Navy's actions in Newport.

Then, when an undercover operative claimed he had a sexual encounter with a highly respected local Episcopal minister, things started to fall apart. The reverend was found innocent, but publicity around his trial introduced the public to the shocking tactics being used by the Navy to catch gay men—sending teens to drug-fueled parties with orders to engage in illegal sex acts. John Rathom, the editor of the *Providence Journal*, wrote a series of news articles demanding an investigation into the Navy's sex sting. His efforts led to Senate hearings in 1921.

During the hearings, the Senate committee condemned the Navy, and especially Roosevelt, for the danger they put the operatives in, and for luring gay sailors to commit crimes, beating and threatening them, and denying them legal representation while in custody. Roosevelt repeatedly denied knowing the details of Arnold's and Hudson's plan, but the Senate committee didn't believe him. Despite all of the controversy, the saga fell quickly out of the public eye because newspapers were reluctant to report all the details of the scandal during those conservative times.

THE AFTERMATH

Ervin Arnold: After the Newport gay sex sting, Arnold faded into obscurity and nothing is known about his post-scandal life.

Erastus Hudson: Hudson was released from the Navy and practiced medicine in New York City while pursuing detective work as a hobby. In the late 1930s, a fingerprinting technique he developed earned him a job as a consultant to the New York Police Department. Hudson entered the spotlight once again when he testified at the trial of Bruno Hauptmann, who was charged with kidnapping the baby of famous aviator Charles Lindbergh (page 50).

Franklin D. Roosevelt: Roosevelt continued to deny having had any knowledge of the Newport sex sting. Regardless of whether or not people believed him, his political career remained intact. He was elected President in 1932, and was reelected twice.

WHY WE STILL CARE

☆ **The scandal introduced mainstream America to gay life and culture.**
The scandal showed mainstream America what a gay community was. Before the scandal, most Americans thought that gay people lived sad and secluded lives in disparate places. But the scandal showed that places existed where gay men came from all over the country to live together in a thriving community, one in which the gay sailors had been welcomed into. Today, of course, there are many well-known gay communities throughout the country, such as Providence in Rhode Island, the Castro district in San Francisco, and Chelsea in New York City.

☆ **It's one of the first well-documented cases on the discrimination toward homosexuals.** The gay soldiers who were caught had been spied on, lied to, beaten, and denied lawyers. While most people back then didn't care much about poor treatment of homosexuals (they saw homosexuals as a threat to the country!), the case does have historical importance in the gay fight for equal rights.

MORE HISTORY ON GAYS IN THE MILITARY

➡ **1778.** President George Washington was the first American to throw a soldier out of the military for being gay—a Lieutenant named Gotthold Frederick Enslin.

➡ **1917.** The US military implemented new Articles of War which stated that any soldier who had (or attempted to have) anal sex would be tried in court.

➡ **1942.** Military psychologists decided that gay people had "psychopathic personality disorders" and that just being gay made a man unfit to be a soldier.

➡ **1993.** During Bill Clinton's presidential campaign, he promised to overturn the military's ban on homosexuals. After becoming President he found out that Congress didn't agree, so he created a new law called "Don't Ask, Don't Tell" as a compromise. This meant that recruits couldn't be asked about their sexuality (don't ask), and that gay service members could remain in the military as long as they weren't openly gay (don't tell).

➡ **2010.** Barack Obama promised in his 2008 campaign for the Presidency that he would repeal "Don't Ask, Don't Tell" within the first 100 days of his presidency. It took a little longer than that, but at the end of 2010, Congress voted to overturn the discriminatory policy thus allowing gay, lesbian, and bisexual service men and women to serve their country openly.

THE SCOOP!

In one of the most shocking events in baseball history, eight members of the Chicago White Sox purposely lost the 1919 World Series to make extra cash.

WHAT WENT DOWN

The 1919 World Series was a showdown between the Chicago White Sox and the Cincinnati Reds. Baseball fans were especially excited about the series because the 1918 season had been cut short due to World War I. To capitalize on the excitement, league officials decided to make the series best-of-nine games instead of the usual best-of-seven.

The White Sox were the favored contenders in the matchup, but the team wasn't happy. Charles Comiskey, the team's owner, had a reputation for paying most of his players poorly, which was starting to piss them off.

One way for the poorly paid players to make a little extra money was to work with the local gamblers who hung around the ball field. By feeding gamblers inside information or throwing a game, a disgruntled player could make as much money from the gamblers as he would in an entire season of playing ball. So, before the World Series, White Sox first baseman Chick Gandil told a gambler buddy that for $100,000 he could make sure the highly favored White Sox lost. That meant anyone betting on the Reds

⚠ THE PLAYERS

➡ Eddie Cicotte, Happy Felsch, Chick Gandil, "Shoeless" Joe Jackson, Claude "Lefty" Williams, Swede Risberg, Fred McMullin
Money-Hungry Chicago White Sox Players

➡ Buck Weaver
Unwilling Participant

➡ Charles Comiskey
Stingy Owner of the White Sox

Swede Risberg making a catch as the White Sox shortstop.

would win big. While the gambler gathered the cash, Gandil got six underpaid teammates to agree to the plan: star outfielder "Shoeless" Joe Jackson, starting pitchers "Lefty" Williams and Eddie Cicotte, shortstop Swede Risberg, outfielder Happy Felsch, and infielder Fred McMullin. Gandil tried to get third baseman Buck Weaver in on the scam, too, but Weaver didn't want any part of it, and he refused to accept any money.

At first, everything went according to plan; the White Sox lost the first two World Series games. But when the gamblers didn't give Gandil and his accomplices the money they were promised, the players got their attention by winning game three. When the gamblers paid up, they made sure the White Sox lost games four and five. But when the gamblers stopped paying again, the

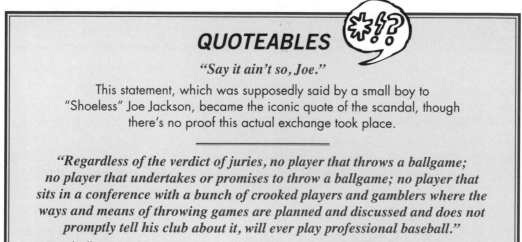

QUOTEABLES

"Say it ain't so, Joe."

This statement, which was supposedly said by a small boy to "Shoeless" Joe Jackson, became the iconic quote of the scandal, though there's no proof this actual exchange took place.

"Regardless of the verdict of juries, no player that throws a ballgame; no player that undertakes or promises to throw a ballgame; no player that sits in a conference with a bunch of crooked players and gamblers where the ways and means of throwing games are planned and discussed and does not promptly tell his club about it, will ever play professional baseball."

Baseball Commissioner Kenesaw Mountain Landis in an official announcement in August of 1921 banning the Black Sox from baseball for life.

crooked players gave up on the plan and won games six and seven, which put the White Sox in a position to win the World Series. One gambler who had a lot to lose if the White Sox won decided to take matters into his own hands. He paid a threatening late-night visit to pitcher Williams and told him bad things would happen to him and his wife if the White Sox won. The next day, the White Sox lost to the Reds 10–5, making the Reds the 1919 World Series champs—and a lot of gamblers very rich.

Though there was plenty of talk that the World Series was fixed, players and owners downplayed it to protect the game's rep, which encouraged more players to throw even more games the next season. By 1920, the game-throwing became so obvious that a grand jury was convened in Illinois to investigate a game the Chicago Cubs allegedly lost on purpose to the last place Philadelphia Phillies. The investigation soon extended to other suspicious games, including those of the 1919 World Series. The grand jury began calling players, owners, managers, writers, and gamblers to testify. Under pressure, Cicotte and Jackson finally 'fessed up to Comiskey about the fix. Comiskey immediately suspended all the crooked players, including Weaver, who hadn't participated in the fix, but knew about it. The eight players were indicted by the grand jury, and Cicotte, Jackson, and Williams all testified they'd thrown the Series. Their confessions made headlines across the country, and forever branded all eight players as the disgraced "Black Sox."

THE AFTERMATH

The Black Sox: In July of 1921, the eight crooked players went to trial for defrauding the public. Luckily for them, all of the records from the grand jury investigation (including transcripts of the confessions of Jackson, Cicotte, and Williams) mysteriously went missing. Without the records, there wasn't enough evidence to convict the players, and they were acquitted of all charges.

The Game: To prevent further gambling and corruption, the position of Baseball Commissioner was created. Kenesaw Mountain Landis, a no-nonsense federal judge, became the first Baseball Commissioner. The day after the Black Sox players were acquitted in 1921, Landis banned all eight players from baseball for life. He wanted to make a point: Acquitted or not, anyone who had anything to do with gambling had no place in baseball.

WHY WE STILL CARE

★ **The scandal created a baseball ban that still stands today.** Any baseball player caught gambling can still be banned from baseball for life and kept out of the Baseball Hall of Fame. Just look at Pete Rose (page 146).

★ **The scandal became the subject of books and movies.** The most famous book, Eliot Asinof's *Eight Men Out: The Black Sox and the 1919 World Series*, was made into the movie *Eight Men Out* starring John Cusack in 1988. W. P. Kinsella's novel *Shoeless Joe*, about a farmer who builds a ballpark in his cornfield where the ghosts of the Black Sox show up to play ball, was turned into the blockbuster movie *Field of Dreams* starring Kevin Costner in 1989.

★ **Baseball fans blamed the Black Sox for future losses.** After the 1919 World Series, the Chicago White Sox went on an 88-year losing streak, which baseball fans called The Curse of the Black Sox. (Their last World Series win was in 1917.) The curse was finally reversed when the White Sox won the World Series in 2005.

MORE BASEBALL CURSES

➡ ***Boston Red Sox.*** When Red Sox owner Harry Frazee sold baseball superstar Babe Ruth to the New York Yankees for about $100,000 in 1920, he saw it as a good business deal. But Red Sox fans saw it as the start of The Curse of the Bambino (Bambino was Ruth's nickname), which kept them from winning the World Series for 86 years.

➡ ***Chicago Cubs.*** In 1945 Billy Sianis, owner of the Billy Goat Tavern in Chicago, bought Cubs tickets for himself and his goat but was told livestock wasn't welcome in Wrigley Stadium. On his way out with his goat, Sianis swore the Cubs would never go to the World Series again. Despite a letter of apology to the goat from the Cubs in 1950 and having a Greek Orthodox Priest bless the dugout in 2008, the hex has held strong.

➡ ***San Francisco Giants.*** When the Giants moved from New York to San Francisco in 1957, they left an important good-luck charm behind, a plaque honoring Giants player Eddie Grant, who died in World War I. Grant's plaque had an honored space at center field in New York, but it got lost during the move. After the move, the Giants played in the World Series nine times but never won. In an attempt to break the curse, an exact replica of the lost plaque was made and hung at ballpark in 2006. It must have worked because in 2010 the Giants won the World Series against the Texas Rangers.

THE SCOOP!

Con artist Charles Ponzi devised a money making scheme that cost thousands of American investors millions of dollars.

WHAT WENT DOWN

Back in the early 1900s, letter writers could include an international reply coupon, which the recipient could use to pay for the return postage. Italian immigrant and con man Charles Ponzi figured out that if you bought a coupon for American return postage in some foreign countries, it could cost less than an actual American stamp bought in the US. His idea was to get people he knew in Europe to send him cheap coupons, trade them in for stamps at a US Post Office, and then sell the stamps at full price, making a profit on the price difference.

He built a company out of this idea and set out to convince people to invest in his international coupon-swapping plan. They'd give him their money to make the coupon trades, and he'd pass down the profits. But Ponzi never actually bought any coupons. Instead, he kept all of the investors' money, and used money from new investors to pay old investors the (fake) profit they were expecting. To make the scam sound legit, Ponzi called his company the Securities Exchange Company, and spread the word around Boston that if you invested in the company you could earn a 50 percent profit in just 45 days.

THE PLAYERS

→ Charles Ponzi
Master Con Artist

→ Thousands of Americans
Those who went broke from the scheme

30

It sounded too good to be true (and it was), but investors lined up anyway. Ponzi even fooled *The Boston Post*, which ran a front-page article about him that said he had doubled investors' money within three months. The article made Ponzi look like a financial genius, and it didn't take him long to rack up thousands of investors. Everyone within 1,000 miles of Boston wanted in on this magical moneymaking scheme—including Ponzi's own wife and eight members of her family. Of course, all the new investors were key to keeping the scam going. As they piled up, Ponzi was pocketing up to $250,000 a day for himself!

Charles Ponzi reading.

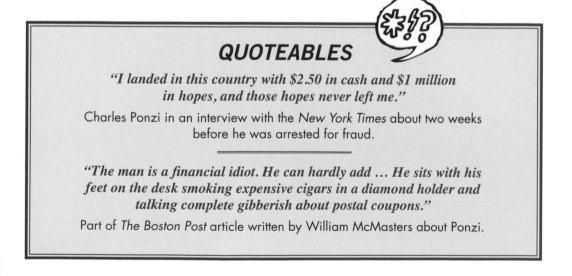

QUOTEABLES

"I landed in this country with $2.50 in cash and $1 million in hopes, and those hopes never left me."

Charles Ponzi in an interview with the *New York Times* about two weeks before he was arrested for fraud.

"The man is a financial idiot. He can hardly add ... He sits with his feet on the desk smoking expensive cigars in a diamond holder and talking complete gibberish about postal coupons."

Part of *The Boston Post* article written by William McMasters about Ponzi.

But the con didn't last long. All of the publicity surrounding Ponzi's scheme had some financial experts and journalists asking questions. And the US Postal Service said it wasn't possible to make the kind of money Ponzi was promising off its coupons. As suspicion spread, *The Boston Post* (which had once done so much to boost Ponzi's business) teamed up with other newspapers in a relentless campaign against him. The US District Attorney's office audited Ponzi's company, forcing him to shut down operations. Then one of Ponzi's employees, William McMasters, turned on him, using evidence he gathered while working for Ponzi to write an exposé about him in *The Boston Post*.

According to McMasters, Ponzi was over $4 million in debt and would never be able to pay off his investors. The government finished its audit just days later and found barely any mail coupons among Ponzi's papers. Instead, the auditor found $7 million in debt, and Ponzi was placed under arrest.

THE AFTERMATH

Charles Ponzi: Ponzi was indicted on 86 counts of fraud by the federal government and spent three-and-a-half years in prison, after which he was released on parole. In 1925, Massachusetts convicted him on state charges, but he escaped to Florida while the verdict was under appeal and tried to make money with a scam selling swampland. He was arrested in Florida but ran away to Texas, then to New Orleans, where he was finally captured and sent back to Massachusetts where he spent nine years in jail. After his release in 1934, he was deported to Italy (where he was from). Reports about the rest of his life vary, but he died at a charity hospital in Rio de Janeiro in 1949.

The Securities Exchange Company: After Ponzi's big scam was revealed, his Securities Exchange Company went out of business and his investors—including his wife and six banks—were wiped out.

The Boston Post: The newspaper won a Pulitzer Prize in 1921 for its investigation of the Securities Exchange Company and its role in Ponzi's arrest.

WHY WE STILL CARE

☆ **The scandal showed how desperate people are to get rich quick.** Ponzi's scheme made no sense—how could you make that much money on postal coupons? But people of all walks of life, both educated and blue collar, handed over their life savings to Ponzi to make a few quick bucks.

☆ **Ponzi's pyramid scheme set a precedent for others.** Ponzi's type of scheme is so well known (and he wasn't even the first to do it), that it's hard to believe that people would still fall for this kind of thing. But they do. The most famous case in recent history is Madoff. In 2008, New York businessman Bernie Madoff was exposed for defrauding thousands of investors—including celebrities, friends, family members, and even charitable foundations—which resulted in a whopping $65 billion in losses.

MORE CON TACTICS

➡ **Boston Red Sox. Pump and Dump.** To pull off this scam, a person buys tons of shares of a really cheap stock, then sends out thousands of (fake) stock advice emails claiming that this stock is about to skyrocket. After you and other investors buy the stock—which will raise its price—the scammer sells his shares for a tidy profit. The stock is still worthless, and investors eventually lose money, but it wouldn't be a scam if they didn't.

➡ **Nigerian 419.** This email scam is named after section 419 of the Nigerian criminal code, which it violates. The scammer starts by sending out tons of emails claiming he's a Nigerian prince or some other kind of overseas rich person and that he needs your help to illegally transfer money out of the country. He says that he'll give you a big chunk of the money in exchange for your bank info and a loan to help pay local bribes and taxes. Of course, he's just stealing your money.

➡ **Identity Theft.** Very simple: The scammer steals your wallet to get your credit card, hacks into your computer to get your bank account information, or convinces you to give personal info via phone or email by pretending to be an employee of a bank or credit card company. If this doesn't work, she can also go through your garbage and use your old bank statements and/or credit card applications to clean out your bank account or open up a credit line in your name.

THE SCOOP!

In 1920, Roscoe "Fatty" Arbuckle was the highest paid star in Hollywood history, but by the end of 1921, accusations of rape and murder ruined his movie career and reputation.

WHAT WENT DOWN

In the early 1900s, Roscoe "Fatty" Arbuckle was a wildly popular silent movie comic, screenwriter, and director. He was nicknamed "Fatty" because of his size, which he often used as a comic asset. By the summer of 1921, Arbuckle had signed a $1 million-per-year contract with Paramount (a ridiculously huge amount of money for the time), and life for him was pretty sweet.

Then, on Labor Day weekend of the same year, Arbuckle and two friends threw a weekend-long party, fueled by tons of alcohol (which was illegal at the time), at the St. Francis Hotel in San Francisco. Among the guests was a small-time starlet and model named Virginia Rappe, who got violently ill during the party. Arbuckle arranged for her to be taken to another room in the hotel so she could recuperate. Multiple doctors were called to check on Rappe, and when she was still sick three days later, she was taken to a nearby hospital. She died three days later. The official cause of death was "rupture of the bladder ... caused by an extreme amount of force." However, after Rappe's death, her friend told the police that Rappe's injuries were a result of being raped by Arbuckle.

THE PLAYERS

→ Roscoe "Fatty" Arbuckle
Superstar Comedian

→ Virginia Rappe
Young Starlet

→ William Randolph Hearst
Newspaper Magnate

"Fatty" Arbuckle in the 1917 short silent film, Coney Island.

Despite the lack of any hard evidence against Arbuckle, the press went absolutely wild over the news. Newspapers (mostly those owned by William Randolph Hearst, see page 114) painted Arbuckle as a lecherous star who raped a defenseless starlet, crushing her internal organs in the process with his considerable heft. The articles gleefully embellished and even fabricated parts of the story to make it more exciting—anything to sell more newspapers. The District Attorney (who wanted to use the publicity around the case to advance his political ambitions) charged Arbuckle with manslaughter. And the public's anger at

QUOTEABLES

"The real essence of this Arbuckle matter, however, is a general lowering of the moral standards in this country."

Neal Dodd, minister of Hollywood's St. Mary of the Angels Episcopal Church, in reference to how he (and many churches) felt the movie industry harmed society.

"Acquittal is not enough for Roscoe Arbuckle. We feel that a great injustice has been done him. We feel also that it was only our plain duty to give him this exoneration, under the evidence, for there was not the slightest proof adduced to connect him in any way with the commission of a crime."

Part of the written apology the jury foreman read after declaring Arbuckle not guilty at his third trial.

Arbuckle was whipped into such fervor that someone shot at his wife in the courthouse.

Despite public outrage, the jury couldn't agree on a verdict during the first two trials, resulting in two mistrials. By the third trial, Arbuckle's films had been banned, his reputation was ruined, and he was deeply in debt. However, at this trial the defense pulled out all the stops: Arbuckle testified movingly, Rappe's character was viciously called into question, and all the circumstantial evidence was discredited. After only six minutes of jury deliberation, Arbuckle was unanimously declared not guilty, and he even received a written letter of apology from the jury. But the damage had already been done.

WHY WE STILL CARE

☆ **Arbuckle left a hefty legacy.** He set the stage for dozens of overweight male comics in years to come like Jackie Gleason, John Belushi, Chris Farley, and Jack Black. He's most often compared to Chris Farley, not only for his size and physical comedy but also for his early, tragic death—Farley died in 1997 at the age of 33 from cardiac arrest caused by a drug overdose. In fact, at the time of Farley's death, he was in talks to star in a biopic of Arbuckle's life. Arbuckle, unfortunately, also set the stage for career-ruining celebrity scandals.

THE AFTERMATH

Roscoe "Fatty" Arbuckle: Though Arbuckle managed a minor directorial comeback years later under the pseudonym William Goodrich, he spent most of his post-scandal life as an alcoholic and an outcast. He died of a heart attack in his sleep in 1933 at only 46 years of age.

Arbuckle's Films: Only a small number of early Hollywood movies that include the comedian's performances have survived, but there was enough footage to release a four DVD collection of his work in 2005. And in 2006, the Museum of Modern Art in New York City programmed a month-long series of his films, so that he could be remembered for his talent, and not just the scandal.

★ **The trial changed the way movies were made.** Even though the alleged incident at the wild party happened off screen, it (along with a few other less famous scandals) got everyone talking about the general lack of morality in the movies themselves, and religious leaders and the public began pressuring the government to censor films. A new set of movie censorship guidelines, known as the Hays Code, banned acts considered immoral at the time from the big screen. In 1968, the Hays Code was replaced with the rating system we use today.

MORE CELEBRITY MURDER DEFENDANTS

➡ **Donnell "Spade" Cooley.** In 1961, when actor and big band leader Cooley's wife asked for a divorce, he answered her by beating her to death. He was convicted of her murder and sentenced to life in prison.

➡ **OJ Simpson.** This Hall-of-Fame football player and actor was accused of murdering his ex-wife and her friend in 1994. The resulting murder trial became an international media sensation and the verdict is still a hot topic of dispute (page 186).

➡ **Robert Blake.** TV and movie actor Blake married Bonnie Lee Bakley in 2000 after DNA tests proved he was the father of her son. A year later, Bakley was found shot and killed in her car outside a restaurant the couple had just left. Though Blake was acquitted on criminal charges, Bakley's other children (from a previous relationship) filed a civil suit against Blake. That jury found him liable for wrongful death and ordered him to pay a $30 million settlement.

➡ **Phil Spector.** Throughout the 1960s, Spector was a wildly successful songwriter and music producer, but by the turn of the 20th century he had become a recluse. In 2003, the body of actress Lana Clarkson was discovered at Spector's home. He insisted she had died of an accidental suicide while handling a gun, but other women began to come forward claiming that Spector had held them in his house at gunpoint. Spector's first trial ended in a mistrial, but in 2009 he was convicted of murder and sentenced to 19 years to life in prison.

THE SCOOP!

Wealthy Chicago boys Nathan Leopold and Richard Loeb confess to kidnapping and murdering 14-year-old Bobby Franks—just to see if they could.

WHAT WENT DOWN

Nathan Leopold and Richard Loeb became friends when they were teenagers. They had a lot in common: They were both brilliant, graduated from college before turning 20, and came from wealthy, respectable families in Chicago's suburbs. It was Leopold, 19, who introduced Loeb, 18, to the 19th-century philosopher Nietzsche's concept of the "superman"—someone born so superior to other men that laws and morality just didn't apply to him.

The boys believed they were supermen. To prove it, Loeb wanted to start committing (and getting away with) crimes. He knew Leopold had a crush on him so they arranged what became known as the "secret compact." Leopold would help out with the crimes, and in return Loeb would provide sexual favors. They started small with arson and robbery. But soon they decided that the best test of their supermen status would be a kidnapping for ransom. They also decided that they'd need to kill their victim to avoid getting caught.

In May of 1924, the boys drove around their neighborhood looking for a victim finally settling on 14-year-old Bobby Franks, a neighbor and Loeb's cousin. They figured Franks'

THE PLAYERS

→ Nathan Leopold
Teen Murderer #1

→ Richard Loeb
Teen Murderer #2

→ Clarence Darrow
Defense Lawyer

→ Bobby Franks
The Victim

Richard Loeb and Nathan Leopold await their verdict in court.

millionaire father could easily afford the ransom, and they knew Franks well enough to convince him to get into their car. After they did, one of them (Leopold and Loeb later blamed each other) hit Franks multiple times in the head with a chisel and jammed a rag down his throat. He died in the back seat of the car.

After the first part of their crime went exactly as planned, they drove Franks' body to the woods, poured acid over any identifying features (like his face), and dumped it into a drainpipe. The boys were ready to move on to the next phase of the plan—their elaborate ransom scheme. But they never got the chance. The police found Franks' body the very next day.

It didn't take long for police to figure out who killed Franks. Leopold had accidentally dropped his glasses right next to the body. Both boys confessed to the crime, and were so proud of their plan, they made sure to describe every detail in their confessions. When the details reached the papers, the public was horrified, and the media went to town with the story of two wealthy teenagers who killed for thrills. Since the boys confessed to everything, there was nothing left for their parents to do but hire the most expensive and famous defense lawyer in the country,

Clarence Darrow (who also represented John Scopes, page 42), and hope for the best.

Darrow focused on keeping Leopold and Loeb out of the electric chair, where most of the country looked forward to seeing them fry. He brought psychiatrists in to study the boys so they could explain why their friendship was such a murderous combination (a genius new defense technique). Darrow then won the judge over with a moving speech at the trial (the judge even cried!). The speech became one of the most famous courtroom closing arguments in history, and it saved the boys from the death penalty. Leopold and Loeb were spared from the chair and sentenced to life in jail for the murder, plus another 99 years for the kidnapping.

THE AFTERMATH

Richard Loeb: Loeb and Leopold remained friends behind bars. The twisted besties even planned to open a school for other prisoners together in jail. But, in 1936, Loeb was killed by a prison inmate who claimed Loeb had been hitting on him.

Nathan Leopold: Leopold published a memoir of his time in prison, *Life Plus 99 Years*,

in 1958. That same year, he managed to get himself paroled after 33 years in prison. After his release, he moved to Puerto Rico where he got married, taught math at a local university, worked as an administrator in a leper colony, and published a scientific book about birds. All the while, he kept a photo of his friend Loeb in a place of honor on his mantle. He died of a heart attack in 1971.

WHY WE STILL CARE

☆ **The murders represent a parent's worst fears.** Just like the teenagers of today, the youth of 1920s Chicago often rebelled against their parents—sneaking out of their houses to go to parties with alcohol, wearing racy clothing, and having casual, premarital sex. Their parents were worried senseless about what would happen to their kids, and Leopold and Loeb confirmed middle-class America's worst fears. Their example still scares parents today.

☆ **Darrow's defense tactic is still used in courtrooms.** During the trial, a very clever Darrow argued that experiences in Leopold's and Loeb's childhoods, along with their exposure in college to Nietzsche's "superman" concept, created a deadly combination that made the crimes they committed inevitable. According to Darrow, if the crimes were inevitable, then the boys couldn't be blamed for carrying them out. Blaming a crime on a bad childhood is a common line of defense used today.

MORE PARTNERS IN CRIME

➡ **Bonnie and Clyde.** From 1932 to 1934, the young couple enjoyed a life together filled with murders, kidnappings, carjackings, and bank robberies. The duo managed to escape the police for years, but their luck finally ran out in Louisiana in 1934, when the police caught up with them, sprayed their car with bullets, and ended their lives.

➡ **The Menendez Brothers.** After watching a mini-series about rich kids killing their fathers, brothers Lyle and Erik hatched a plan to kill their own dad. They thought he was controlling, plus he was threatening to cut them out of his will. They decided to murder their mom, too, to save her the pain of losing him. In August of 1989, the brothers snuck into their parents' Beverly Hills mansion and shot them both dead. The brothers were eventually arrested, and, during their famously televised trial in 1993, claimed they committed the murders because their parents had sexually molested them. The jury didn't buy it, and they were sentenced to life in prison.

➡ **Eric Harris and Dylan Klebold.** More commonly known as the Columbine Killers, Harris and Klebold marched into their high school in April of 1999 and shot 37 classmates and teachers, killing a total of 13 people before turning their guns on themselves. As bad as that sounds, their original plan was worse. They had planted bombs in the cafeteria to blow up the whole school, but when the bombs failed to explode, they were forced to switch to Plan B—the shooting spree.

THE SCOOP!

A Tennessee law that banned teaching the theory of evolution in the classroom resulted in a highly publicized showdown between two lawyers about science and religion.

WHAT WENT DOWN

Scientist Charles Darwin developed the theory of evolution way back in the 1800s. He believed that every living thing on earth started as a single-cell organism and developed over millions of years to become what it is today. According to his theory, humans descended from ape-like beings millions of years ago. And a lot of scientists agreed with him. But Christians who believed that God created the world in six days (also called creationists) strongly disagreed.

In March of 1925, the state of Tennessee decided that it would settle the argument by passing the Butler Act, which prevented teachers from teaching anything in Tennessee schools that denied "the story of the Divine Creation of man as taught in the Bible." Passing the act was really just a way to make a point: Tennessee was pro Bible. No one planned to arrest any teachers. But the American Civil Liberties Union (ACLU), an organization with a mission to protect citizens' constitutional rights, saw the Butler Act as a violation of teachers' freedom of speech. The ACLU placed ads in Tennessee newspapers looking for a teacher willing to break the new law, and the organization promised to pay any subsequent court fees and fines. The ACLU's plan was for the

THE PLAYERS

➡ John Scopes
Evolution Defending
Science Teacher

➡ William Jennings Bryan
State of Tennessee's
Creationist Attorney

➡ Clarence Darrow
Scopes' Agnostic
Attorney

Scopes' attorneys, including Clarence Darrow (at right) at the famous trial.

teacher to go to trial, argue against the Butler Act, and hopefully get it overturned.

With all the controversy surrounding the Butler Act, it became obvious that the trial would bring a lot of publicity (and money) to the town in which it was held. Town leaders in Dayton, Tennessee, convinced local high school science teacher John Scopes to break the new law so the trial could be held in Dayton. As planned, Scopes was arrested by police and put on trial. The trial quickly became known as the Scopes Monkey Trial (since Darwin said humans were descended from apes), and it was front-page news nationwide just like the people in Dayton hoped it would be.

QUOTEABLES

"If today you can take a thing like evolution and make it a crime to teach it in the public school … At the next session you may ban books and the newspapers. Soon you may set Catholic against Protestant … and try to foist your own religion upon the minds of men."

Clarence Darrow explaining why the Butler Act was unconstitutional during the Scopes Trial.

"I am simply trying to protect the word of God against the greatest atheist or agnostic in the United States!"

William Bryan on the witness stand, defending the Bible against Darrow's endless questions about its validity.

The trial was so huge that downtown Dayton was closed off to traffic to accommodate the media circus, tourists, and vendors selling food, drinks, and monkey souvenirs. Chicago's WGN radio even arranged to broadcast the trial live—a first in US history. The frenzy attracted two superstar lawyers: William Jennings Bryan, a staunch antievolution crusader who represented Tennessee; and Clarence Darrow (who also represented Leopold and Loeb, page 38), a famous agnostic lawyer and theory-of-evolution champion, who defended Scopes.

The trial was supposed to be about whether or not Scopes violated the Butler Act, but it turned into a dramatic showdown between the two lawyers on the Bible vs. Science. The highlight of the trial was when Darrow called his opponent, Bryan, to the stand to testify as a Bible expert. Darrow grilled him with questions about the accuracy of the Bible like, "When exactly was the earth created?" and, "How many days did it take?" The judge asked Darrow to stop his line of questioning, while Bryan responded by pounding his fists and claiming he was protecting the word of God. The theatrics (and the trial) lasted eight days, though the jury only needed nine minutes to find Scopes guilty. His punishment: a $100 fine.

WHY WE STILL CARE

☆ **People are still fighting over what to teach in schools.** Up until the 1980s, it looked like the theory of evolu-

THE AFTERMATH

The Trial: After losing the trial in Dayton, the ACLU took the case to the Tennessee Supreme Court on appeal, hoping to get it overturned. The Supreme Court decided that the Butler Act was constitutional, but in 1927, it overturned the Scopes verdict on a technicality. In 1955, *Inherit the Wind*, a play based loosely on the trial, opened on Broadway. A movie adaptation was released in 1960, and it was nominated for four Academy Awards.

The Law: Tennessee repealed the Butler Act 1967. In 1968, a similar law in Arkansas was declared unconstitutional by the US Supreme Court. In 1987, the Supreme Court also struck down a Louisiana law that required schools to teach creationism along with evolution, saying it violated the separation of church and state.

tion would prevail. Even the Supreme Court cited the separation of church and state as a reason to keep the creationist theory out of the classroom. But creationists then lobbied to have "intelligent design" taught in schools along with evolution. According to intelligent design, life on earth is just too complex to have developed randomly over time, and must be the work of a higher intelligence. The argument is ongoing: Creationists continue to say that intelligent design is not about religion, while opponents continue to say that it's just religion in disguise.

The Scandal showed the effects that a trial could have on a town. Dayton benefitted greatly from hosting the trial. It brought publicity and money to the town, and it's still famous for it. But these days, media coverage is so huge, big trials can be more of a burden than a benefit to the cities where they take place. Months of extra security, garbage pick-up, and additional electricity can cost a city a lot of money. For instance, LA County spent over $9 million on OJ Simpson's murder trial, one of the most widely covered trials in history (page 186).

MORE ACLU COURT CASES

➡️ **Brown vs. the Board of Education.** In 1954, Oliver Brown along with 12 other African American parents, argued that having separate schools for black and white kids went against the Equal Protection Clause in the 14th Amendment. The ACLU backed them up, and the Supreme Court ruled in favor of Brown, forcing all American schools to integrate.

➡️ **Loving vs. Virginia.** As recently as 1967, it was illegal in Virginia (and 15 other states) for a black person and a white person to get married. But the ACLU helped already married couple Mildred and Richard Perry Loving fight for their right to live as husband and wife. The Supreme Court put an end to race-based legal restrictions on marriage in Virginia—and everywhere else in the country.

➡️ **Roe vs. Wade.** Before 1973, it was illegal in most states for a woman to get an abortion unless the pregnancy put her life in danger. That was the case in Texas where Jane Roe wanted to terminate a pregnancy but couldn't. The ACLU helped take her case to the Supreme Court, saying her right to privacy under the 14th amendment included the right to decide when and if to have children. In what's still thought to be a very controversial case, the Supreme Court agreed with Roe, putting an end to all the state laws making abortion illegal.

THE SCOOP!

Italian immigrants Nicola Sacco and Bartolomeo Vanzetti were put on trial for stealing $15,000 and murdering two men. The only thing the prosecution could prove was that they were immigrants with radical views about abolishing government—but that was enough to cost them their lives.

WHAT WENT DOWN

A payroll master and his security guard were murdered in South Braintree, Massachusetts, in April of 1920 while delivering $15,000 to a shoe company. Witnesses told police that the two gunmen "looked like Italians." At the time, anarchist groups who opposed America's capitalist government (and had many Italian immigrant members) were on the rise on the East Coast. Some of the more radical members voiced their opinions by sending pipe bombs in the mail to politicians, rich industrialists, judges, and other authority figures. The police suspected that the Braintree murder was the work of Italian radicals and went on a hunt for suspects.

THE PLAYERS

➡ Nicola Sacco
Italian Anarchist #1

➡ Bartolomeo Vanzetti
Italian Anarchist #2

They picked up two Italian anarchists: Nicola Sacco, a shoemaker, and Bartolomeo Vanzetti, a fish peddler. The police based their arrest on the fact that the men were connected to a car that may have been at the scene of the crime. Vanzetti also had an announcement for an anarchist rally in his pocket. Plus, both men were armed when they were arrested, and Sacco's gun was the same kind as the one used in the murders (though it wasn't necessarily the same gun). The suspects contradicted themselves repeatedly under police interrogation, which made them seem guilty, though this could have been because they barely spoke

English. In the end, the evidence was thin, the men had no criminal history, and none of the stolen money was found anywhere near them. Still, they were put on trial for the robbery and murder.

A Sacco-Vanzetti Defense Committee was formed by supporters of the anarchists, and California lawyer Fred H. Moore was hired to lead the defense, while a district attorney led the prosecution. The trial, which was supposed to be about the murder, focused more on Sacco's and Vanzetti's beliefs. The prosecution asked them question after question about their anarchist views (they believed a capitalist government was an unfair system), why they had escaped to Mexico to avoid being drafted for World War I (they didn't believe in war), and whether or not they loved America (they did—except for how capitalism hurt the working classes). Their views were considered

Public protests of the executions at New York City's Union Square, 1927.

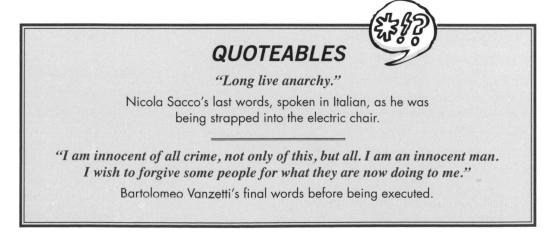

QUOTEABLES

"Long live anarchy."

Nicola Sacco's last words, spoken in Italian, as he was being strapped into the electric chair.

"I am innocent of all crime, not only of this, but all. I am an innocent man. I wish to forgive some people for what they are now doing to me."

Bartolomeo Vanzetti's final words before being executed.

unpatriotic and dangerous. Although there was no solid evidence linking them to the crime, both men were found guilty and sentenced to death.

The verdict sparked instant outrage from Sacco and Vanzetti supporters worldwide. They thought the trial was unfair and that two innocent men were being railroaded into the electric chair by the US justice system because they were immigrants with radical political views. Thousands gathered for marches and protests in working class neighborhoods in the US and in Europe (especially in Italy), and bombs were sent to American embassies in Europe in protest. The governor of Massachusetts received death threats along with hundreds of letters asking for clemency for the men, including 22 letters from members of the British parliament.

The case stayed in the news for six years while Sacco and Vanzetti waited on Death Row. Big-shot lawyers (including future Supreme Court Justice Felix Frankfurter) searched for new evidence and worked tirelessly to get them a new and fair trial. But the judge—Webster Thayer—refused a new trial, making many think he had it in for Sacco and Vanzetti from the start. When all the possible appeals were exhausted, and amid tremendous protests, Sacco and Vanzetti were sent to the electric chair in August of 1927 in Charlestown State Prison, Massachusetts.

THE AFTERMATH

The Execution: After Sacco's and Vanzetti's execution, 7,000 people marched in an eight-mile funeral procession in Boston while nearly 200,000 people looked on. As news of the execution spread, so did protests—from general worker strikes in Sweden and Argentina, to riots in Switzerland where 5,000 people invaded downtown Geneva and smashed store windows. Smaller riots took place in London, Hamburg, and Berlin. Five thousand people tried to attack the US Embassy in Paris, sending 124 police and almost 500 rioters to the hospital. In 1977, to commemorate the 50th anniversary of the men's execution, Massachusetts Governor Michael Dukakis issued a proclamation saying that Sacco and Vanzetti didn't receive a fair trial. Dukakis also named August 23 (the day of their executions) a day of memorial for the men, despite much objection from the state legislature.

☆ **The scandal reminded Americans of the importance of due process.** According to the US Constitution, the government must respect the rights of its citizens, and one of those rights is the right to a fair trial. This is known as due process. Whether Sacco and Vanzetti were involved in the South Braintree robbery or not, the reason so many people were outraged was because they believed the two men didn't get a fair shake. They were put on trial despite a lack of evidence and were found guilty (and put to death) mainly because they were radicals who had critical views of the US.

☆ **The case is an example of how the US has been quick to condemn people connected with a radical way of thinking.** In the late 1600s, Americans put so-called witches on trial and burned them at the stake; in the 1920s, it was Sacco and Vanzetti for their anarchist views; and in the 1950s, anyone with connections to communism, which resulted in the famous Rosenberg trial (page 66).

MORE AMERICAN ANARCHIST HISTORY

➡ ***Haymarket Riot 1886.*** When police tried to break up a labor rally led by anarchists in Chicago's Haymarket area, a bomb was thrown at the police. After the explosion and subsequent police gunfire, about a dozen people were dead, and about 100 more were wounded. Local anarchists were then rounded up by police for questioning, and 8 were put on trial for murder. Though there was little evidence linking any of them to the bomb, all 8 were convicted and 7 were sentenced to death.

➡ ***President William McKinley Assassination 1901.*** Republican President McKinley was at an exhibition in Buffalo, New York, when anarchist Leon Czolgosz shot him twice in the chest. Czolgosz said he shot the President (who died of gangrene a week later) because the President was an enemy of the working people. Czolgosz was put on trial and sentenced to death.

➡ ***World Trade Organization (WTO) 1999.*** The WTO (a global organization that promotes free trade) attracted almost 50,000 protestors when it met in Seattle. Black-clad anarchists were front and center, breaking chain-store windows, slashing police cruiser tires, and generally disrupting the conference. The National Guard had to be called in, and by the time it was over, police made 500 arrests and $9 million worth of damage was done to the city.

THE SCOOP!

Charles Lindbergh was famous for being the first man to fly a plane nonstop across the Atlantic. But in 1932, he became even more famous when his 20-month-old baby was kidnapped and found murdered. The result was a highly publicized trial that ended with a man in an electric chair.

WHAT WENT DOWN

In 1927, Charles Lindbergh became the first person to complete a flight across the Atlantic Ocean, flying from New York to Paris. Before Lindbergh's successful flight, people traveled the route by boat, which took a week! Lindbergh became a hero and spent the following years traveling in his plane, the Spirit of St. Louis, and giving speeches about the awesomeness of air travel.

Five years later, Lindbergh was settled in New Jersey with a wife and baby (Charles, Jr.), but he was still a huge celebrity. So when little Charles was kidnapped from the Lindbergh's home in March of 1932, the public followed every step of the police search. The kidnapper left a poorly written ransom note demanding $50,000. Another note demanding $70,000 arrived in the mail a week later. Then, a third note was sent demanding an intermediary be used in the baby–cash exchange. People all over the country offered to help, including retired high school principal John Condon, who put an ad in *The Bronx Home News* offering himself as an intermediary. The kidnapper sent a letter to Condon's house the very next day approving

☂ THE PLAYERS

➡ Charles Lindbergh
Celebrated Aviator

➡ Charles Lindbergh, Jr.
Kidnapped Baby

➡ Bruno Richard Hauptmann
Convicted Kidnapper

➡ John Condon
Volunteer Go-Between

The Cleveland Press
HOME EDITION

REVEALS KIDNAPERS KILLED BABY AND THEN TOOK $50,000

TRICKERY OF GANGS EXPOSED

WORLD'S SYMPATHY GOES TO THE LINDBERGHS

OFFICIAL CITES 'SLEEPER' CLEW

A newspaper clipping about the scandal.

late-night meetings between Condon and the kidnapper in cemeteries, Condon handed over $50,000 in gold notes (an old form of paper money backed by real gold bars) to the kidnapper in exchange for instructions on where to find Charles, Jr. The police had recorded the serial numbers on the gold notes so they could trace them, which was a good thing since the instructions didn't lead to the baby. A month later, Charles, Jr.'s body was discovered in the woods near Lindbergh's house. A coroner's examination showed the baby died from a fatal blow to head soon after he was kidnapped.

The case was such a big deal that in September of 1933, President Roosevelt put the FBI in charge of finding the kidnappers, and issued a proclamation demanding that all gold notes be brought to the Treasury so when the gold

him as the official go-between and instructing Condon to communicate with him through the classifieds in the local newspaper.

After more ransom notes, weeks of negotiations though classified ads, and multiple

QUOTEABLES

"I hope you boys will excuse me, but I would rather the State Police answered all your questions, I am sure you understand how I feel."

Charles Lindbergh to reporters shortly after his baby's kidnapping.

"Dear Sir, Have 50,000$ ready ... After 2–4 days we will inform you were to deliver the Mony. We warn you for making anyding public or for notify the Polise the child is in gut care ..."

Part of the first badly written ransom note found at the kidnapping scene.

notes from the ransom were returned, they could be traced back to the kidnappers. The plan worked! In September of 1934, the FBI traced some gold notes back to a German-born Bronx ex-con named Bruno Hauptmann. When the FBI searched Hauptmann's home, more than $13,000 worth of gold notes with serial numbers matching the ransom money were found in his garage.

Hauptmann was charged with murder, and the public was sure he was guilty. Newspapers reported every detail of the case and 60,000 curious on-lookers flooded into the small town of Flemington, New Jersey, where the trial was held. At the trial, handwriting experts testified that Hauptmann had written all of the ransom notes. Eyewitnesses also claimed he was the same man Condon had handed the ransom money to in the cemetery, and FBI forensics tests showed that wood from the ladder used in the kidnapping matched the wood of Hauptmann's attic floor. But no one had actually seen the kidnapping or murder, and there was no hard evidence—like fingerprints—to prove Hauptmann was guilty. Still, Hauptmann was found guilty of murder in the first degree and sentenced to death. He died in the electric chair in April of 1936.

THE AFTERMATH

Bruno Hauptmann: There were questions about Hauptmann's guilt long after his death. Some critics felt the media had convinced the public Hauptmann was guilty and even argued that evidence had been tampered with to make him seem so. In 1982, Hauptmann's widow, Anna, sued the state of New Jersey for $100 million claiming the execution was unjust, but the lawsuit was dismissed.

Charles Lindbergh: Lindbergh moved his family to Europe in 1935. He visited Germany in 1936 and, after World War II began, moved back to the US with some very controversial views. He claimed that the US shouldn't be fighting against countries made up of white people and spoke out against Jews in American culture and politics. His anti-Semitic beliefs ended his hero status, though he remained famous for his achievements in the air and won the Pulitzer Prize in 1954 for his book, *The Spirit of St. Louis*, an account of his famous flight

★ **The trial shows how public opinion can influence a trial.** The American public loved Lindbergh and desperately wanted to see someone punished for his son's death. Hauptmann's arrest was big news and every piece of evidence against him was played up in the papers until the whole world was convinced he'd committed the murder before the trial even began. The jury was only presented with circumstantial evidence, and there was no evidence that placed Hauptmann at the scene of the crime. Still, he was sentenced to death.

★ **It was one of the first cases to use forensics to help solve a crime.** Today it's common for DNA evidence, fingerprints, and even tiny pieces of fibers to be used as hard proof, but this was all new stuff in the 1930s. The FBI opened its first crime lab (like *C.S.I.*, but more low-tech) in 1932. Analyzing the handwriting in the ransom notes and examining the ladder found at the Lindbergh kidnapping scene were among its first (and most famous) projects.

MORE FAMOUS KIDNAPPINGS

➡ *Frank Sinatra, Jr. (1963).* The 19-year-old son of the famous singer was nabbed from his Lake Tahoe hotel room where he was preparing for a performance that night. The kidnappers demanded just $240,000 from Frank senior who, with help from the FBI, got his son back safely. One of the kidnappers turned himself in a couple days later, and the rest of the kidnappers were in custody soon after. At the trial, the kidnappers' defense argued that Frank, Jr. had orchestrated the kidnapping for publicity, but nobody bought it and all the men were convicted.

➡ *John Paul Getty, III (1973).* Getty was 16 when he was abducted from his apartment in Rome. When a $17 million ransom note reached his billionaire grandfather (and the police), they thought it was a hoax the teenager was playing to make some cash. When they received his severed ear in the mail, they changed their tune, eventually handing over almost $3 million to the kidnappers. Soon after, Getty was found alive on the side of the road.

➡ *Patty Hearst (1974).* The granddaughter of the super wealthy newspaper magnate William Randolph Hearst was abducted from her Berkeley apartment at gunpoint by the radical group the Simbionese Liberation Army (SLA). At first police and Hearst's family did everything they could to get her released, but after a few months in captivity, the SLA started releasing audiotapes of Hearst calling her parents pigs and claiming she'd joined the group willingly (page 114).

THE SCOOP!

Glamorous Gloria Morgan Vanderbilt fought her dead husband's powerful family for custody of her only daughter *and* access to her daughter's $5 million trust fund in a media circus trial that revealed her bad girl behavior.

WHAT WENT DOWN

When 45-year-old millionaire Reginald Claypoole Vanderbilt died suddenly in 1925, he left behind a 20-year-old wife (Big Gloria), a baby girl (Little Gloria), and a lot of debt. Once the debt was paid off, Big Gloria was left with a lot less money than she had expected. She was used to the finer things in life and a lump some of $130,000 wasn't going to cut it. Her daughter, however, was left with a $5 million trust fund. But Big Gloria was considered by the court to be a minor, which meant she wasn't old enough to be given full guardianship of her daughter or her daughter's money. However, the court did award her a $4,000 per month allowance to support Little Gloria. Big Gloria spent most of that money (and most of her time) partying around Europe with her twin sister, Thelma, and other rich and fabulous friends. She took Little Gloria with her all over Europe, though the little girl was often left with her nanny or grandmother, who were also in tow.

Reginald's rich sister, Gertrude Vanderbilt Whitney, never liked Big Gloria, and she really didn't like how Little Gloria was being raised. So, in 1932, after Little Gloria had

THE PLAYERS

➡ Gloria Morgan Vanderbilt (Big Gloria)
Wealthy Heiress

➡ Gloria Vanderbilt (Little Gloria)
Her Daughter

➡ Reginald Claypoole Vanderbilt
Deceased Dad

➡ Gertrude Vanderbilt Whitney
Disapproving Aunt

Little Gloria, 10, with her mom after the court granted custody to her aunt.

her tonsils removed in a New York hospital, Whitney suggested that Little Gloria stay with her at her Long Island estate so the girl could recuperate. Little Gloria remained at the estate for the next two years. When Whitney told the judge overseeing the Vanderbilt case that Little Gloria was now living with her, the court threatened to cut Big Gloria's monthly payments (which were obviously not going to childcare) down to $9,000 per year.

Suddenly, Big Gloria wanted Little Gloria back. She moved home to New York City and set herself up in a mansion on the Upper East Side, where Little Gloria could come to visit. In September of 1934, during one of those visits, Little Gloria, then 10, went to Central Park with her nanny and never came back. She'd been whisked back to Whitney's mansion on Fifth Avenue,

QUOTEABLES

"We lived in Paris for four and a half years and during that period my daughter paid absolutely no attention to little Gloria … Usually she slept until 1 or 2 o'clock in the afternoon and from that time until the early hours of the following morning she was at cocktail parties, dinners, and night clubs."

Part of the affidavit presented by Big Gloria's own mother to the court in 1934.

"I kept saying to myself that when I grow up, I'll marry and have a lot of children and I'll love them so much that they'll never be unhappy."

Little Gloria in an interview with *Time* magazine in 1942 recalling her feelings during the custody trial.

where she was kept under constant guard. When Big Gloria realized what had happened, she was furious. She claimed her daughter had been kidnapped and immediately petitioned the court to get her back. Suddenly Little Gloria was in the middle of a giant custody battle and highly publicized trial—a welcome distraction to Americans who were smack in the middle of the Great Depression. Crowds waited outside the courthouse every day to catch a glimpse of Little Gloria, who became known as the "poor little rich girl," and newspapers reported every juicy detail.

Whitney found it easy to prove that Big Gloria was an unfit mother. Chauffeurs, nannies, and even Big Gloria's own mom testified to all kinds of bad-girl behavior—partying till dawn, drinking before breakfast, reading "dirty books," and lots of sleeping around. Her maid even testified to finding her in bed with another woman, a revelation that was so shocking in the 1930s the judge immediately closed the courtroom to the public and the press to keep the case under control. In the end, the judge decided to take Little Gloria into his chambers and ask her who she wanted to live with. Little Gloria chose Whitney, and the judge ruled in her favor, though he did award Big Gloria with visits on weekends, Christmas, and the month of July.

THE AFTERMATH

Big Gloria: Big Gloria spent two more years fighting to win custody of her daughter, going all the way to the Supreme Court but with no luck. Relations between the two Glorias became frosty. When Little Gloria turned 21 and got control of her own inheritance she cut Big Gloria off. By then Big Gloria had opened a dress shop in New York with her twin sister, Thelma, and had some money of her own.

Little Gloria: Little Gloria lived on her Aunt Whitney's estate until her first marriage, at 17, to Hollywood agent Pat DiCicco. She divorced him four years later and married three more times: at 21 to conductor Leopard Stokowski, at 32 to director Sydney Lumet, and (finally) at 39 to writer Wyatt Cooper. She also wrote many books, including *Once Upon a Time*, a memoir about her childhood, and *It Seemed Important at the Time: A Romantic Memoir*, which was a graphic sexual account of her affairs with famous men like Howard Hughes, Marlon Brando, and Frank Sinatra. But she's probably most famous for her line of Gloria Vanderbilt jeans and for being the mom of CNN news anchor Anderson Cooper.

WHY WE STILL CARE

⭐ **The scandal showed money can cause misery.** The Vanderbilts were so rich that they were like American royalty, and the country looked to them with a sense of awe and jealousy. That is, until people saw how the money tore the family apart in the end, and ruined a little girl's childhood.

⭐ **The trial raised questions about motherhood.** At the onset of the custody battle most of the public believed there was no better place for a kid than with her mother and that that's where Little Gloria should stay. But as revelations about Big Gloria's hard partying and neglectful ways leaked out of the courthouse, views began to change. The public soon realized that maybe not all mothers were naturally nurturing. Now it's easier for us to see that some moms might not be the best influence in their children's lives.

MORE CUSTODY BATTLES

➡ **Woody Allen and Mia Farrow.** The two were a New York power couple until Allen started dating Farrow's 21-year-old adopted daughter Soon-Yi Previn, in 1993. Farrow had 11 children in all (three with Allen), and she wasn't about to give Allen custody of any of them when they split. She even accused him of molesting her adopted daughter Dylan, who was seven at the time. The judge agreed that he was a terrible father and gave her custody of all kids. Allen and Previn married in 1997.

➡ **Britney Spears and Kevin Federline.** Spears married backup dancer KFed in 2004 after knowing him for three months. They had two kids but divorced in 2007. In the bitter, public custody fight that followed, Spears became known for her new hard partying, no-panty-wearing lifestyle. She lost custody of her boys after failing to comply with a judge's orders to go to parenting classes and agree to drug tests. In the end, KFed got full custody (and $20,000 a month in child support), while Spears was allowed two overnight visits a week.

➡ **Anna Nicole Smith's Lovers.** Former *Playboy* model and reality-TV star Anna Nicole Smith was famous for her marriage to an elderly billionaire, and the $1.6 billion he left her in his will. When Smith died of an accidental overdose in 2007, several men claimed to be the father of her five-month-old daughter, who was the sole heir to Smith's fortune. A year of court cases and one DNA test later, Smith's ex-boyfriend Larry Birkhead turned out to be the lucky—and now very wealthy—dad.

ORSON WELLES' RADIO SHOW CONVINCED COUNTRY THAT ALIENS WERE INVADING 1938

THE SCOOP!

Director Orson Welles created a scary Halloween radio show that was made to sound like a real-time space invasion. He was only trying to entertain the public, but he wound up creating a nationwide panic.

THE PLAYERS

- Orson Welles
  Radio Show Creator
- CBS Radio
  Station That Aired the Show
- New York and New Jersey Residents
  Panic-Stricken Listeners

WHAT WENT DOWN

In the spirit of Halloween, small-time director Orson Welles and his team of writers decided to present a radio version of H. G. Wells' 1898 novel *War of the Worlds* for *The Mercury Theater on the Air*, a CBS radio program that broadcasted hour-long dramas each Sunday. The novel was about an alien invasion in London set before the turn of the 20th century, but Welles was afraid the story would be too boring and unbelievable for American audiences. To make it more exciting, he had the writers set the story in New Jersey, and he presented it as a series of news bulletins that would interrupt music, just like real breaking news. Before the show began, the station announced it was all fake, but many listeners missed the disclaimer.

The first "news bulletin" was an interview with an astronomer, played by Welles, who claimed he'd seen bursts of incandescent gas on Mars. Later, there was a report of a huge flaming object crashing down on a farm in Grovers Mill, New Jersey. Then, an actor playing an on-scene reporter described

Orson Welles being interviewed about his radio show gone wrong, 1938.

aliens with tentacles and skin like wet leather emerging from a spaceship.

As the fake Martians incinerated the fake crowd on the radio, real pandemonium broke loose all over the country—especially near the supposed alien landing site. While the broadcast described aliens pulling down bridges, spraying poison gas all over New Jersey, and crossing the East River to kill everyone in New York City, 20 families in Newark, New Jersey, ran into

QUOTEABLES

"There, I can see the thing's body. It's large as a bear and it glitters like wet leather. But that face—it—it's indescribable. The eyes are black and gleam like a serpent. The mouth is V-shaped with saliva dripping from its rimless lips that seem to quiver and pulsate."

The fake on-scene reporter describing the aliens as they emerge from their fake spaceship during the *War of the Worlds* broadcast.

"Far from expecting the radio audience to take the program as fact rather than as a fictional presentation, we feared that the classic H. G. Wells fantasy … might appear too old-fashioned for modern consumption."

Orson Welles in a statement apologizing for the panic caused by the *War of the Worlds* broadcast and insisting that it wasn't intentional.

"I heard that broadcast and almost had a heart attack. I didn't tune it in until the program was half over … I ran out into the street with scores of others and found people running in all directions. The whole thing came over as a news broadcast and in my mind it was a pretty crummy thing to do."

Bronx resident Lewis Winkler relating his experience to a *New York Times* reporter the day after the broadcast.

the streets with wet towels wrapped around their faces like gas masks. Other listeners hid in their basements, packed their cars with valuables, headed to church, or frantically called friends and relatives, spreading the panic even further.

From coast to coast, police switchboards, newspaper offices, and CBS headquarters were overwhelmed with frenzied calls for help and information. The show started at 8 pm and by 9 pm, the panic was so wide-spread that the Associated Press had to release a statement that the broadcast was just a show and not real news. When everyone realized that they'd been listening to a story and not a live report, they were embarrassed and pissed. Newspapers relished in the chaos that its new media rival (radio) had created, and were especially hard on Welles, who had to spend a lot of time post-broadcast apologizing to the American people.

THE AFTERMATH

The Radio Show: Welles and *The Mercury Theater on the Air* cast were detained and questioned by police directly after the broadcast, but no arrests were made. The Federal Communications Committee (FCC) launched an investigation into the matter but couldn't figure out what (if any) laws had been broken. In the end, CBS got a slap on the wrist and had to promise to be more careful in the future.

Orson Welles: The scandal turned Welles into a household name. At the time, the 23-year-old was well known but only in the theater world. After his radio scare, the entire world knew his name, which helped him transition to a career as a successful movie director. His most famous movie, *Citizen Kane*, is considered by most to be one of the greatest movies ever made.

☆ **The panic raised questions of whether radio needed more regulation.** In 1938, radio was new, exciting, and powerful. It could deliver news much faster than newspapers and had the power of sound, which could add drama and emotion. The panic caused by the *War of the Worlds* broadcast had critics worried that radio was too immediate and powerful, and needed stronger regulation to make it safe. Similar to talk about the internet now.

☆ **The incident showed that people are prone to mass hysteria.** In addition to the three disclaimers during the broadcast that the show was a work of fiction, there were many obvious clues that aliens weren't really coming. As word spread, though, so did the panic, which usually happens when people are so blinded by fear they can't see the truth.

MORE EXAMPLES OF POINTLESS MASS HYSTERIA

➡ **The Mad Gasser of Mattoon.** The residents of Mattoon, Illinois, were convinced that someone was squirting noxious gas into homes in the summer of 1944. But no one could possibly have gotten to all the households that complained of nausea, swollen throats, and even temporary paralysis. As reports of attacks increased, so did the hysteria around them; one night 17 homes on one street claimed to be attacked. No culprit was ever caught and no chemicals were ever discovered in any of the homes.

➡ **Alien Attack, Part 2.** In 1949, a radio station in Quito, Ecuador, used the *War of the Worlds* template to broadcast a similar invasion-from-Mars story, but with much more tragic consequences. The frightened mob, which had run into the street in panic about the attack, turned their fear into rage after learning the broadcast was a hoax. They stormed the building that housed the radio station and set it on fire, killing 20 people and injuring many more.

➡ **April Fool's Day in Jordan.** To celebrate April Fool's Day in 2010, the *Al Ghad* newspaper in Jordan ran a front page report of a UFO landing outside the city of Jafr. Unfortunately, the people of Jafr weren't in on the joke. Parents pulled their kids from school, and the mayor even sent a security team out to search for the aliens, which almost caused an evacuation of the town.

THE SCOOP!

Comedian Charlie Chaplin was one of America's most loved movie stars until Joan Barry, his 22-year-old stalker ex-girlfriend, slapped him with a paternity suit and claimed he was her baby's daddy.

WHAT WENT DOWN

From the 1920s to 1940s, Charlie Chaplin wrote, produced, directed, and acted in some of early Hollywood's most influential films. He made millions of people laugh with his portrayal of "The Little Tramp"—a funny-walking clown with a mini moustache, bowler hat, and cane. Off-screen, he had a personal life that involved a different kind of mischief: affairs with women half (or a third) his age. But it wasn't until he met 21-year-old Joan Barry that Chaplin's troubles really began.

Chaplin was 52 when he met Barry in the summer of 1941. She wanted to become a movie star, so he offered her a $75-per-week contract with his studio and promised her a role in an upcoming film. He also started an affair with her. Their relationship was on and off for the next two years, and, as time went by, Barry's crazy side started to show. Sometimes she'd get drunk and drive to Chaplin's house at night. One time, she crashed her car in his driveway; another time, she broke a window in his house when he wouldn't open the door for her.

One night in 1942, things got really bad. Barry broke into Chaplin's house and ran up to his bedroom waiving a gun. She demanded to know why he hadn't called her and threatened to kill herself in his house to cause a scandal. By that time, her contract with Chaplin's studio was up, so he calmed her

⋀ THE PLAYERS

➤ Charlie Chaplin
Famous Film Star

➤ Joan Barry
Unhinged Girlfriend and
Would-Be Starlet

down by offering to pay her $25 per week if she would just put down the gun and go to sleep in the other room. Later, Barry claimed that after giving up the gun they had sex, but Chaplin insisted they didn't.

Barry left peacefully the next day, but she was arrested a week later for vagrancy when police found her in her car outside Chaplin's house, only partially dressed and with iodine smeared on her face. She was given a 90-day sentence that was suspended on the condition that she leave Los Angeles. So she did. Chaplin probably hoped that was the end of their crazy relationship. But it wasn't. Barry broke in to his house again a few months later to tell him she was pregnant, the baby was his and was conceived the last time they'd seen each other. Chaplin responded to the news by having Barry thrown back in jail.

Charlie Chaplin in his 1940 movie, *The Great Dictator.*

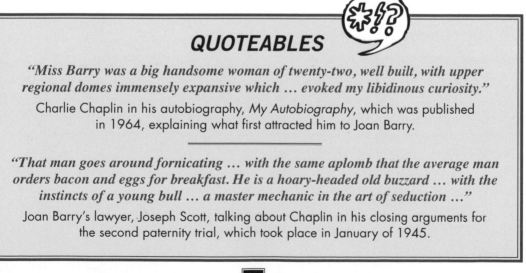

QUOTEABLES

"Miss Barry was a big handsome woman of twenty-two, well built, with upper regional domes immensely expansive which ... evoked my libidinous curiosity."

Charlie Chaplin in his autobiography, *My Autobiography*, which was published in 1964, explaining what first attracted him to Joan Barry.

"That man goes around fornicating ... with the same aplomb that the average man orders bacon and eggs for breakfast. He is a hoary-headed old buzzard ... with the instincts of a young bull ... a master mechanic in the art of seduction ..."

Joan Barry's lawyer, Joseph Scott, talking about Chaplin in his closing arguments for the second paternity trial, which took place in January of 1945.

Chaplin insisted it was impossible that he could be her baby's dad and insisted Barry was only after his money. Barry stuck to her story, and worked to get the media on her side. She spilled her guts to Hollywood gossip columnist Hedda Hopper—a smart choice since Hopper hated Chaplin. In Hopper's eyes, Chaplin was a lecherous villain who promised a young and impressionable girl a career in the movies only to knock her up, have her arrested, thrown out of town, and arrested again. Hopper devoted all her time to hyping the scandal. Smelling a payout, Barry's mother got involved and with her daughter filed a paternity suit against Chaplin. At first, Chaplin agreed to pay child support and pay Barry's legal expenses as long as she agreed to a blood test after the baby was born to prove the truth once and for all. When the blood tests proved he wasn't the dad, Chaplin thought it would be the end of the drama. But Barry and her mom pushed through with the paternity suit claiming the blood tests were wrong.

Blood tests back then weren't as accurate as DNA evidence is now, and they couldn't be used as evidence in California court cases. So all Chaplin had was his word, which wasn't much because of his rep as a heartless womanizer. Barry's lawyers used Chaplin's bad rep to their advantage in the two trials that followed and without the blood test as proof, Chaplin lost the paternity suit. He was forced to pay $75 a week in child support until Barry's kid turned 21.

THE AFTERMATH

Charlie Chaplin: The US government, who was already after Chaplin for supporting communism, put him on trial for violating the Mann Act, a law that made it illegal to take a female across state lines for "immoral purposes." (He paid Barry's travel expenses to New York to visit and sleep with him.) But they failed to get a conviction. In 1952, Chaplin traveled to Europe for a vacation and was denied admittance back into the US until he proved his "moral worth." He and his wife moved to Switzerland, where he lived until his death in 1977. He returned to the US once, in 1972, to receive an Academy Award. The standing ovation for him lasted five minutes.

Joan Barry: Joan Barry moved to Pittsburgh to become a nightclub singer. She eventually got married and had two more children, but was institutionalized in 1953 after she was found wandering the streets barefoot holding a pair of baby shoes while repeating, "This is magic."

WHY WE STILL CARE

☆ **Charlie Chaplin fans still have a difficult time reconciling the star's on-screen talents with his real-life womanizing ways.** Chaplin helped build the foundation for today's big movie industry. He started his own movie studio (United Artists, which is still in business today) and won Oscars for acting, original screenplay, and even musical scoring. But he's most remembered for the silly "Little Tramp" persona he played in so many of his movies, which seems so out of place with his rep as a womanizer who loved (and left) so many young girls.

☆ **Chaplin's paternity case changed laws.** The legal community thought it was totally unfair that Barry could win a paternity case when blood tests proved Chaplin wasn't the father of her kid. As a direct response to the case, laws were changed so that blood tests were admissible in California courts, and the changes spread to other parts of the country. Now DNA tests can determine paternity with 99.99 percent accuracy, so what happened during Chaplin's paternity trial will likely never be repeated.

MORE OF CHARLIE CHAPLIN'S WOMEN

➡ **Mildred Harris.** A child star, Harris was also Chaplin's first wife. A pregnancy scare forced the couple to get married in 1918, when she was 16 and he was 29. That pregnancy was a false alarm, but they later had one child together. Unfortunately, the baby died. And so did their marriage, in 1920, after just two years.

➡ **Lita Grey.** Grey was given a leading role in Chaplin's movie *The Gold Rush* in 1924, when she was 16, but was dropped from the film when she got pregnant with Chaplin's baby. He married her to avoid scandal, and they had another child together, but their marriage ended in a very public, nasty divorce in 1926.

➡ **Paulette Goddard.** An accomplished actress, Goddard met Chaplin in 1936 on the set of his movie *Modern Times*; she was 21. Like many of Chaplin's leading ladies, she became his girlfriend, and they may or may not have gotten married on a trip to Asia. (They were notoriously secretive about their relationship.) Their relationship lasted six years, but they broke up right before Joan Barry entered the picture.

➡ **Oona O'Neill.** The 18-year-old O'Neill married Chaplin against the wishes of her father (famous playwright Eugene O'Neill) in 1943. She gave birth to the first of their eight children during Chaplin's paternity trials. And the couple's age difference (36 years!) helped add to Chaplin's bad rep as a perverted old man. However, Chaplin and O'Neill remained happily married until his death in 1977.

THE SCOOP!

A nationwide FBI hunt for American spies who helped the Soviets develop the atomic bomb led to the highly publicized trial of Julius and Ethel Rosenberg, the first civilians put to death for espionage.

WHAT WENT DOWN

In 1949, the US was in the middle of a Red Scare, meaning most Americans (especially those in government) were terrified of Communists and the Soviet Union. When the US government found out that the Soviets had figured out how to make an atomic bomb (which only the US had been able to do so far), J. Edgar Hoover, the head of the FBI, was convinced the Soviets had help from Americans who were secretly spying for them.

Bent on figuring out who was revealing our nuclear secrets, Hoover sent the FBI on a rampage to arrest and interrogate any American who was suspected of spying for the Soviet Union. The massive investigation eventually led the FBI to David Greenglass, an Army man stationed in Los Alamos (where the US had developed the world's first atomic bomb). During the interrogation, Greenglass admitted to the FBI that he had passed information to the Soviets. He also pointed the finger at his brother-in-law, Julius Rosenberg.

Rosenberg was a member of the Communist Party in the US and, according to Greenglass, was heading up a Communist spy ring, which he convinced Greenglass to join. Greenglass admitted that he passed some handwritten notes and sketches of a high-explosive lens

THE PLAYERS

➡ Julius Rosenberg
Small-Time Spy #1

➡ Ethel Rosenberg
Julius' Wife

➡ David Greenglass
Small-Time Spy #2

➡ Morton Sobell
Small-Time Spy #3

➡ J. Edgar Hoover
Head of the FBI

nold to Rosenberg, and the FBI used Greenglass' confession to arrest Rosenberg and Morton Sobell (another member of the spy ring who had unsuccessfully tried to flee to Mexico) in the summer of 1950.

Ultimately, the FBI just wanted Rosenberg to admit he was a spy and give the FBI the names of his other spy friends. But Rosenberg refused. So the FBI moved to Plan B and arrested Rosenberg's wife, Ethel, to make him change his mind. But that plan backfired. Rosenberg still wouldn't confess. In the end, Julius, Ethel, and Sobell were all charged with conspiracy to commit espionage—a capital crime that could get them the death penalty. All three pled not guilty.

Greenglass, on the other hand, struck a deal with the FBI to get a lighter sentence (and keep his wife from being prosecuted). As part of the deal, he pled guilty to espionage and he and his wife, Ruth, testified against the Rosenbergs and Sobell at their trial. The Greenglasses' testimony against

Ethel and Julius Rosenberg in prison.

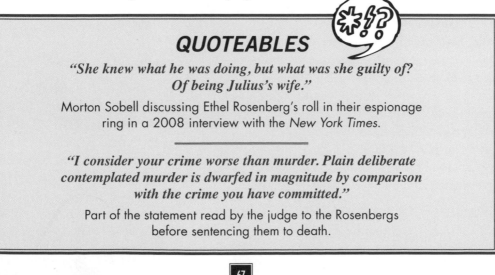

QUOTEABLES

"She knew what he was doing, but what was she guilty of? Of being Julius's wife."

Morton Sobell discussing Ethel Rosenberg's roll in their espionage ring in a 2008 interview with the *New York Times*.

"I consider your crime worse than murder. Plain deliberate contemplated murder is dwarfed in magnitude by comparison with the crime you have committed."

Part of the statement read by the judge to the Rosenbergs before sentencing them to death.

Ethel (that she supposedly typed some spy notes for Julius) was the only evidence against her. However, other spies' testimonies against Julius and Sobell were much more convincing. The jury quickly came back with a guilty verdict for all three of them. Sobell was sentenced to 30 years in prison, but the Rosenbergs' sentence was much worse: Death.

When the public learned of the Rosenbergs' sentence, many people were outraged. Despite the outcome of the trial, a lot of people believed they were innocent. And even if they were guilty, the death penalty seemed like an extreme punishment, especially since Ethel's role in the spy ring was still unclear, and they had two small children. As the Rosenbergs waited for their turn on the electric chair, they became symbols of government abuses brought about by fear of Russia and Communism. Thousands of supporters marched in protest to stop the execution, and letters flooded the White House. The Rosenbergs' lawyer, Emanuel Bloch, spent two years making appeals to spare the couple's lives, taking the case all the way to the Supreme Court. Still, in June of 1953, Julius and Ethel were put to dealth by electric chair in Sing Sing prison. They were the first American citizens ever executed for espionage.

THE AFTERMATH

The Case: The Rosenbergs' kids were adopted by family friends. As adults, they got involved in a decade-long legal battle to get the FBI, CIA, and Justice Department to release documents they said would clear their parents' names. But as documents were released and key players in the Rosenberg trial started coming forward, the brothers finally concluded in 2008 that their dad really was a spy.

Morton Sobell: Also in 2008, Sobell admitted to the *New York Times* that he and Julius were in the spy ring. However, Sobell also insisted Ethel was innocent.

David Greenglass: Greenglass was released from prison in 1960. In 2001, he admitted to Sam Roberts, author of the book *The Brother: The Untold Story of Atomic Spy David Greenglass and How He Sent His Sister, Ethel Rosenberg, to the Electric Chair,* that he lied about Ethel's involvement to keep his own wife from being prosecuted as a spy. He now lives under an assumed name and claims he doesn't feel guilty about what he did because the Rosenbergs could have avoided the electric chair if they had just admitted to espionage.

WHY WE STILL CARE

☆ **The scandal is an example of government abuse, big time.** It's now obvious that the only reason Ethel was arrested was to put pressure on Julius to confess. To make matters worse, she was put on trial and sentenced to death based on evidence prosecutors got by offering a deal to Ethel's brother and sister-in-law. Officials now even admit that they used the threat of the death penalty for Julius and Ethel as a last ditch effort to get them to finally admit to the spying and give up any information they had. And to justify their death sentences, the government led the public to believe that the Rosenbergs had actually sent the Soviet's instructions on how to make the bomb—even if they didn't.

☆ **The Rosenbergs were the first civilians executed for espionage in United States history.** The punishment for the Rosenbergs crimes may seem unnecessarily harsh. More recently convicted spies whose espionage has led to dozens of deaths (see sidebar) have gotten off with just jail time. But during the Rosenbergs' sentencing, Americans' fear and hatred of Communism was so strong that the judge believed they deserved the maximum punishment.

MORE CONVICTED SPIES

➡ ***Nathan Hale.*** At the start of the Revolutionary War in 1776, George Washington asked for a volunteer to go behind enemy lines and find out what the British were planning. Spying was considered an ungentlemanly activity back then and 21-year-old Hale was the only one ungentlemanly enough to do the deed. Hale made it past enemy lines, but the British figured out what he was up to and hung him before he could get any info back to the patriots.

➡ ***Aldrich Ames.*** In 1957, 16-year-old Ames joined the CIA, and was a loyal employee, until he became strapped for cash and started selling the names of American spies working in the Soviet Union to the Soviets for around $50,000. He later received a salary of $300,000 for continuing to supply Soviets with classified information. He sold out about 25 of his CIA friends in all, some of whom were executed by Soviet authorities. It took the CIA almost 10 years to figure out that Ames was a mole; he was finally caught in 1994 and sentenced to life in jail.

➡ ***Robert Hanssen.*** An FBI agent who was trained to catch spies, Hanssen was sharing highly classified national security information with the Soviets for more than 20 years. He was finally caught in 2001. Hanssen ended up with a life sentence in the same minimum-security prison as Aldrich Ames, which ruined his original plan of moving to Moscow to teach courses in espionage.

ROCK SINGER ELVIS' SEXY HIP-SHAKING ON TV SHOCKS THE NATION

1956

THE SCOOP!

Elvis Presley took rock 'n' roll mainstream in the 1950s, but when he shook his hips during a performance on prime-time TV, everyone from American parents to the Pope demanded he stop polluting teens' minds with his sexy shenanigans.

WHAT WENT DOWN

Elvis Presley came on to the scene in the 1950s with hit songs like "Heartbreak Hotel" and "Hound Dog." He brought rock 'n' roll music to the mainstream by mixing up a combo of gospel, R&B, rockabilly, and pure sex appeal. Teenagers worldwide instantly fell in love with him and his music, and he soon became known as the King of Rock. But the 1950s were a conservative time and Elvis' music and moves frightened parents, who were convinced that rock 'n' roll would lead directly to premarital sex, juvenile delinquency, and rioting.

Despite his critics, Elvis wasn't seen as a big threat until 1955, when he signed with major music label RCA, which wanted to get into the rock 'n' roll biz and planned to make a fortune off of Elvis' popularity—and his good looks. Girls were going bonkers over the hot young rock star in his tight-fitting clothes, greased-up hair, and bad-boy sideburns. But it was the way he danced that really drove the ladies wild. Adults found his thrusting, swiveling hips especially threatening, earning him his second most famous nickname, "The Pelvis" (which was supposed to be an insult), while the press mainly portrayed him as a classless, talentless hick.

THE PLAYERS

➡️ Elvis Presley
Sexy Rock 'n' Roller

➡️ Milton Berle, Steve Allen, and Ed Sullivan
TV-Show Hosts

All of the negative attention just made Elvis an even bigger star. By 1956, he had three number-one hits and was selling records like crazy. When he appeared on *The Milton Berle Show* in June of 1956, it was a TV event no one would ever forget. Elvis had performed on TV before, but he usually kept things tame with a slow song. That night, he took things up a notch and sang his hit "Hound Dog" while gyrating his hips and sneering sexily at the audience. His act would get a PG rating today, but back then it was considered shockingly sexual. Even the Roman Catholic Church joined the anti-Elvis chorus with an article in its weekly magazine *America* warning people to "Beware Elvis Presley."

The backlash was almost enough to get Elvis' next TV appearance—this time on *The Steve Allen Show*—canceled. To calm everyone's

Elvis Presley shaking his hips on The Milton Berle Show, 1956.

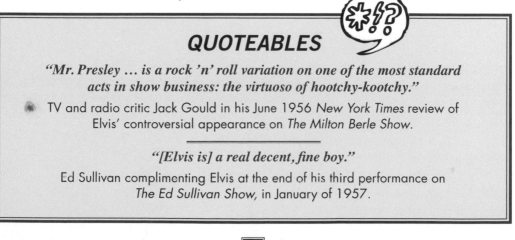

QUOTEABLES

"Mr. Presley ... is a rock 'n' roll variation on one of the most standard acts in show business: the virtuoso of hootchy-kootchy."

TV and radio critic Jack Gould in his June 1956 *New York Times* review of Elvis' controversial appearance on *The Milton Berle Show.*

"[Elvis is] a real decent, fine boy."

Ed Sullivan complimenting Elvis at the end of his third performance on *The Ed Sullivan Show,* in January of 1957.

fears, Allen had Elvis dress up in a top hat and tuxedo instead of his controversial skintight clothes, and had him sing "Hound Dog" to an actual basset hound, which sat droopily on a pedestal. The show's ratings soared. More than 55 percent of the American TV audience tuned in, giving *The Steve Allen Show* more viewers than its rival, *The Ed Sullivan Show,* for the first time in history.

Ed Sullivan was not happy. Though he vowed never to have Elvis on his show because Elvis was so vulgar, Sullivan ate his words and shelled out $50,000 (a shocking sum back then) for Elvis to perform on *The Ed Sullivan Show* three times. In Elvis' first appearance, he sang "Don't Be Cruel" in front of a live audience in Hollywood. But cameramen for *The Ed Sullivan Show* never showed anything below Elvis' waist in an attempt to censor his sexy dancing. Ironically, this only called more attention to the dancing as the television audience wondered what the camera wasn't showing every time the live audience screamed. By the time Elvis made his third (and last) appearance on *The Ed Sullivan Show*, it was clear that music—and TV—would never be the same again.

THE AFTERMATH

Elvis' Career: Elvis' success skyrocketed after his wildly popular appearances on TV. His first movie, *Love Me Tender*, made back its entire production cost after just three days in the theater. He had to take a short break from stardom in 1958 when he was drafted to the Army, but over the 20 years that followed, he starred in more than 30 films and released more than 90 albums. For decades, he also held the record for the artist with the most top-100 hit singles in the history of the Billboard Hot 100 chart (he had 108), but the cast of the TV Show *Glee* finally beat him in February of 2011 (they had 113).

Elvis' Personal Life: The King married Priscilla Beaulieu in 1967. Their daughter, Lisa Marie Presley, was born a year later, but their marriage ended in 1973. After the divorce, Elvis gained a lot of weight and became addicted to prescription drugs. In August of 1977, at 42, he was found dead lying on his bathroom floor. The official cause of death was listed as cardiac arrhythmia (an irregular heartbeat), but his autopsy showed 14 different drugs in his system. Graceland, Elvis' mansion in Memphis, Tennessee, was opened to the public in 1982, and it still attracts more than 600,000 visitors each year.

WHY WE STILL CARE

☆ **Elvis created the look for rock 'n' roll.** He was a great musician, but it was his image people will always remember: His bad-boy style, slinky moves, and exaggerated sexuality. Rock stars today still follow in his footsteps, combining massive sex appeal with their acts.

☆ **Elvis started the teen heartthrob trend.** A huge part of why Elvis became so wildly popular was that he tapped into the fervent fandom of teenage girls. Once the music industry caught wind of how much money teen girls were willing to spend on their musical crushes, it created more moneymaking dreamboats. Every generation since has had its own Elvis, from David Cassidy to Justin Timberlake to Justin Bieber.

MORE CONTROVERSIAL MUSIC ACTS

➡️ **Madonna's "Like A Prayer" Video.** In 1989, Pepsi signed a multi-million dollar deal with Madonna (page 158) to debut the title track for her new album, Like A Prayer, in a Pepsi commercial. Pepsi spent weeks building hype around the G-rated commercial. But the day after the commercial premiered, MTV premiered the real video for "Like A Prayer"—complete with a rape scene and flaming crosses. This pissed off religious groups and Pepsi; the company never aired the commercial again.

➡️ **Justin and Janet at the Super Bowl.** Janet Jackson and Justin Timberlake performed together in the Super Bowl XXXVI half-time show in 2004. At the end of a song, Timberlake reached over and pulled part of Jackson's costume off, exposing her right boob.

Though Justin did the ripping, it was Jackson who apologized. She blamed a "wardrobe malfunction," though people didn't believe it. In fact, the country was so shocked, Jackson was uninvited from the Grammys that year and the Federal Communications Commission fined CBS $550,000.

➡️ **Adam Lambert at the American Music Awards (AMA).** American Idol runner-up Lambert began his 2009 AMA performance on ABC by dragging two almost-naked men across the stage by a leash, after which another man pretended to give Lambert oral sex. He then took a brief break from his song to make out with his male keyboard player. After the performance, outraged viewers flooded the Federal Communications Commission and ABC with complaints. Lambert, however, felt no need to apologize. He said that people only found his performance obscene because he is a gay man, and that if he had been a hot young female pop star, people would have loved it.

THE SCOOP!

Confidential was the first magazine to expose the real dirt on Hollywood celebrities. Its gossipy articles pissed off famous actors and movie studios and led to a six-week court case with an all-star cast.

WHAT WENT DOWN

There was a time when big movie studios like MGM and Paramount had control over the press and were able to keep any negative news about their movie stars under wraps. If a reporter wrote something the studios didn't like, that reporter was banned from press conferences, movie sets, and one-on-one interviews. There were gossip magazines, but they needed permission from studios to run their stories. But that time ended when Robert Harrison launched *Confidential* magazine in 1952 and figured out how to get the real scoop—without asking permission.

Harrison's vision for *Confidential* was that no Hollywood star or story was too big to be off-limits. Harrison ran the magazine from New York but sent his niece to LA to put together a group of spies—made up of private investigators, hotel bellhops, call girls, and celebrity wannabes armed with mini cameras and hidden recording devices—to get the dirt on celebrities for the stories. They were paid to hang around stars and catch them misbehaving. The magazine's favorite topics were cheaters, homosexual affairs (homosexuality could ruin a career), and interracial affairs (also a

THE PLAYERS

➡ Robert Harrison
Founder of Confidential Magazine

➡ Pat Brown
Hollywood-Friendly California Attorney General

➡ Howard Rushmore
Disgruntled Ex-Editor of Confidential

A typical issue of *Confidential* from the 1950s.

big deal since interracial marriage was still illegal in most states). Its first issue sold 250,000 copies, and before long it became the best-selling magazine on newsstands with a circulation of almost four million.

Hollywood stars and movie studios hated *Confidential* for ruining their perfectly maintained images, but they didn't know how to shut Harrison up. They couldn't pay him off because he was making tons of money, and they couldn't kick him out of Hollywood because he wasn't there. Some celebrities tried suing him for libel (writing a lie about a person that you know will be damaging), but most of those lawsuits went nowhere because none of the celebrities wanted to go to court. Then, in 1957, pressure from Hollywood big shots prompted California Attorney

QUOTEABLES

"What is really disturbing, is the discovery that the [US], despite free public education and a high literacy rate, contains so many morons who will support these gamey magazines."

Columnist Inez Robb in an August 1955 article expressing her dismay at *Confidential's* success.

" ... behind the scenes, [Desi] Arnaz is a Latin Lothario who loves Lucy most of the time but by no means all the time. He has, in fact, sprinkled his affections all over Los Angeles for a number of years. And quite a bit of it has been bestowed on vice dollies who were paid handsomely for loving Desi briefly ... "

Part of an article from the January 1955 issue of *Confidential* claiming TV star Desi Arnaz was cheating (with prostitutes!) on his famous comedian wife, Lucile Ball.

General Pat Brown to put a stop to the magazine once and for all. With testimony from Howard Rushmore, a disgruntled former editor at *Confidential*, Brown was able to charge Harrison and 10 associates with conspiracy to commit libel and conspiracy to publish obscene material. All of Hollywood cheered Brown on, but the celebration was short lived.

Harrison's lawyers made sure that if Harrison was going to be sued for printing lies, every star *Confidential* wrote about would have to appear in court to prove the stories were fake. Celebrities panicked over having to talk about their bad behavior under oath and many tried to leave town before Harrison's legal team could serve them with subpoenas. The case became known as the "Trial of 100 Stars," and every newspaper and magazine was there to cover it. After six weeks of titillating testimony, the jury couldn't decide if *Confidential* was guilty. There should have been a second trial, but no one involved wanted to relive the drama (including Harrison), so a deal was made outside the courtroom: The state of California would drop all charges, if *Confidential* and Harrison agreed to stay out of stars' private lives for good.

WHY WE STILL CARE

☆ **Confidential showed the world that celebrity gossip could be big business.** Thanks to *Confidential*, it didn't take long for other magazines to see just how much money there was to be made from Hollywood scandals.

THE AFTERMATH

Confidential: The magazine died from lack of gossip. No one wanted to read the scandal-free, post-trial version of the magazine. Circulation fell from four million to approximately 200,000. Harrison sold the magazine in 1958, and it continued to struggle along until 1978, when it finally closed its doors.

The Hollywood Celebs: Hollywood studios lost the power to cover up celebrity scandals. Though *Confidential* wasn't allowed to dish gossip anymore that didn't mean nobody could. Dozens of new scandal mags popped up in its place, and now there were too many enemies to fight. The studios no longer had control over their stars' images and stars no longer had a right to a private life.

When *Confidential* folded, other tabloids were there to take its place, giving rise to today's multi-million-dollar celeb gossip industry, which includes magazines like *Star, OK!, Us Weekly,* and the *National Enquirer*, not to mention TV shows like *The Insider* and websites like TMZ.

☆ **The scandal taught stars to use gossip in the press to their advantage.** *Confidential* didn't only ruin careers, it offered stars an opportunity for big publicity. Celebrities (or celebrity wannabes) would leak juicy, but not ruinous, stories about themselves, knowing millions of eyes would be reading the mag each month. Celebrities use the same tactics now, informing paparazzi about where they're going to be and releasing carefully chosen gossip just as a movie, book, or TV show is about to come out.

MORE GOSSIP MAGS PUT ON TRIAL

➡ *Carol Burnett vs. the* **National Enquirer.** In 1976, the *National Enquirer* reported that legendary comedian Burnett got into a drunken argument with Secretary of State Henry Kissinger during dinner at a Washington, DC, restaurant, and then traipsed around the dining room offering random diners a bite of her dessert while knocking over wine glasses. Burnett furiously denied the incident. She spent the next decade suing the *Enquirer* and finally won $200,000, inspiring more celebrities to sue the magazine.

➡ *Britney Spears vs.* **Us Weekly.** While pop princess Spears was married to Kevin Federline, she tried to sue *Us Weekly* for an article about a supposed sex tape the couple had made together. Spears argued that *Us Weekly* was ruining her rep by merely mentioning such a tape existed, but a judge disagreed, saying that since she had basically built her career around her sexuality, the mention of a sex tape couldn't possibly ruin her rep, and she lost the case.

➡ *Brangelina vs.* **News of the World.** In January of 2010, when the British tabloid *News of the World* reported that the power couple was calling it quits, dividing their millions, and planning custody of their six kids, Brangelina struck back with a lawsuit. They forced the tabloid to admit that the divorce attorney they quoted had never even met them and demanded that the magazine print a retraction and fork over an undisclosed amount of money in damages. They won the case and didn't seem to mind at all when news spread that they donated their winnings to charity.

THE SCOOP!

Jerry Lee Lewis was one of the hottest rock 'n' roll stars in the 1950s, but when English tabloids found out he married his 13-year-old cousin, his rep quickly went down the tubes.

WHAT WENT DOWN

Jerry Lee Lewis was a talented musician and rock 'n' roll pioneer. He met Myra Gale Brown in 1956 when he moved in with his cousin, J. W. Brown. Myra was J. W.'s 12-year-old daughter (making her Lewis' first cousin once removed), and she immediately caught the eye of the 22-year-old rising rock star. He didn't seem to care about the age gap, the fact that they were related, or that he was still married to his second wife, Jane. Within six months, the two were hot and heavy. In December of 1957, Lewis convinced Myra, who was then 13, to secretly cross state lines to Mississippi (where the age restrictions for marriage were lax), and get hitched. At first Myra's parents were pretty pissed about the wedding, but since Myra's father played in Lewis' band, they eventually got over it.

THE PLAYERS

➡ Jerry Lee Lewis
Bad Boy Rock Star

➡ Myra Gale Brown
Lewis' Underage Wife
(and Cousin)

While Lewis was busy romancing Myra, big things were also happening in his music career. He was leading a new rock 'n' roll revolution along with other musical super stars like Elvis Presley (page 70). Lewis—who was nicknamed "The Killer"—was considered the wildest performer of the bunch. He put on crazy, high-energy shows, and once lit his piano on fire and played while it burned.

His 1957 hit single "Whole Lot of Shakin' Goin' On" sold six million copies, but it was banned from many radio stations because encouraging women to "shake baby shake" was considered scandalous back then. His next hit, "Great Balls of Fire," was an even bigger success, and led to a string of hits over the next year as well as a starring roll in *High School Confidential*, a movie named after one of his songs.

Myra stayed out of the spotlight for a little while, and they kept their marriage on the down low. But five months after they got married, Lewis insisted on bringing his young wife with him on a six-week rock tour through England. This decision went against the advice of his manager, who

Jerry Lee Lewis and his 13-year-old wife, Myra, in London.

QUOTEABLES

"I can assure you that my wife is all woman, even though she looks kinda young."

Jerry Lee Lewis trying to convince the crowd of reporters at Heathrow Airport in 1958 that Myra was old enough to be his wife.

"Go home baby snatcher! … Go wheel your wife in a pram!"

An angry audience to Jerry Lee Lewis during his first London show in 1958, after the public learned that his wife was 13.

knew British tabloids would have a field day if they found out about the unconventional relationship. Sure enough, as soon as the couple arrived in London, they were greeted by hoards of reporters. One asked Myra who she was, and she innocently replied that she was Lewis' wife. The news (and her youth) shocked the crowd. Lewis tried to reassure reporters by telling them his wife was 15, but adding two years to Myra's real age still didn't make her old enough.

It also didn't take long for reporters to find out the truth—including the fact that the two were cousins and were married months before Lewis finalized his second divorce. The audience booed and heckled Lewis at his first London show and called him "baby snatcher." His next two shows were just as bad. After the third show, the tour was cancelled, and Lewis' rising career came to a grinding halt.

THE AFTERMATH

Jerry Lee Lewis: After the London debacle, no one wanted anything to do with Lewis. All his interviews and concerts were canceled and radio stations refused to play his songs. Lewis did make a comeback in the late 1960s, this time on the country charts, and released 30 country hits. He was inducted into the Rock 'n' Roll Hall of Fame, with other rock 'n' roll pioneers like Elvis Presley and Chuck Barry, the very first year it opened in 1986.

The Marriage: Lewis and Myra remained married for 13 tumultuous years. Their marriage was seen as proof of the lewd immorality of rock 'n' roll stars and their music. Though Lewis never publicly blamed Myra for ruining his career, their relationship was marred by abuse and the tragic death of their three-year-old son, Steve Allen, who drown in the family's pool. Myra wrote a book about their marriage in 1982 called *Great Balls of Fire: The Uncensored Story of Jerry Lee Lewis*. It was later made into a film starring Dennis Quaid and Winona Rider as Lewis and Myra.

☆ **The scandal shined a spotlight on underage marriage.** Age-of-consent laws for marriage vary from state to state, and in the 1950s it was perfectly legal to get married at 13 in some states. Today, both people must be at least 18 or get the permission of a parent or judge in most US states. (The age of consent for Mississippi is 21, and in Nebraska it's 19.) Though Lewis and Myra's marriage didn't directly change any laws, it brought attention to the issue of underage marriage.

☆ **People still wonder if we missed out on some great music.** Even though many thought it was gross that Lewis married his 13-year-old cousin, his fans—and music critics—have often stated that the world of music suffered by shutting Lewis down right when he was really starting to cook.

MORE KISSING COUSINS

➡ **Charles Darwin and Emma Wedgewood.** The man who gave us the theory of evolution married his cousin Wedgewood. Since he was a scientist, he made a list of pros and cons to decide if he should ask for her hand. On the pro side, she offered better companionship than a dog; on the con side, he'd be forced to visit her relatives. He didn't seem to be bothered, though, that they were related.

➡ **Franklin D. Roosevelt and Eleanor Roosevelt.** FDR, the only President to be elected to three terms in office, and Eleanor, a champion for human rights, were distant cousins. They got married in 1905, and, because they were relatives, she didn't even have to change her last name when she got married.

➡ **Edgar Allan Poe and Virginia Eliza Clemm.** The dark poet met his future bride and cousin, Virginia, when he moved in with his aunt in 1831. He was 20 when he fell in love with her, and she was 7. But being the gentleman that he was, Poe waited until she was 13 to make Virginia his wife.

➡ **Rudy Giuliani and Regina Peruggi.** Giuliani, who would go on to become the mayor of New York City, thought he was marrying his third cousin when he said, "I do" to Peruggi in 1968. They didn't think that was too bad, but after 14 years of marriage, they found out they were actually second cousins, which was apparently too close for comfort. The couple split in 1982 and had their marriage annulled soon after.

THE SCOOP!

Johnny Stompanato, the gangster boyfriend of Hollywood sex symbol Lana Turner, threatened the lives of both Turner and her teenage daughter Cheryl Crane during a violent fight. Cheryl then stabbed him to death sparking a highly publicized investigation.

THE PLAYERS

➡ Lana Turner
Movie Star and Mom

➡ Cheryl Crane
Turner's Teenage Daughter

➡ Johnny Stompanato
Turner's Sometimes Boyfriend

WHAT WENT DOWN

In the 1940s and '50s, Lana Turner was a famous actress and Hollywood sex symbol. She was nicknamed "Sweater Girl" for her form-fitting sweaters, and she took full advantage of her fame by dating a long list of eligible bachelors, seven of whom she married. Turner's only child, Cheryl Crane, was the product of a nine-month second marriage to famous restaurateur Stephen Crane. (The marriage ended before Cheryl was born.) While being Turner's daughter certainly had its advantages, Cheryl's life wasn't all ponies and pool parties at the country club. Turner's lifestyle also brought an element of danger.

In 1957, Turner started a whirlwind romance with bad-boy gangster Johnny Stompanato. Their romance ran hot for a while, but Turner eventually got bored. When she tried to break things off, Stompanato got violent. He strangled her during arguments and threatened to cut her face with razors. During one famous fight in 1958 on a movie set in London, Turner's co-star Sean Connery (the future James Bond) ended up punching Stompanato out. Afterward Turner had the gangster thrown out of England.

Back in the US one year later, the couple, still together, had another violent argument at

Turner's house. She tried to end the relationship (again), but Stompanato threatened to kill her along with then 14-year-old Cheryl and anyone else Turner cared about. Cheryl heard everything from her bedroom. Afraid for her mom's life and her own, she ran to the kitchen, grabbed a butcher knife, and ran back upstairs. When Stompanato stepped out of Turner's bedroom still spewing threats, Cheryl stabbed him in the stomach, severing an artery in his kidney. He died within minutes.

After the incident, Turner called her mother (who sent two doctors to the scene) and a lawyer. Cheryl called her father. The doctors pronounced Stompanato dead, and Cheryl was quietly brought to the Beverly Hills police

Lana Turner, Johnny Stompanato, and Cheryl Crane on vacation two weeks before Stompanato was murdered.

QUOTEABLES

"Then I hear him say, 'I'll get you if it takes a day, a week or a year. I'll cut your face up. I'll stomp you. And if I can't do it myself I'll find somebody who will—that's my business.'"

Cheryl Crane in a police statement on the night of the murder, recalling what Stompanato said right before she stabbed him.

"He grabbed me by the arm and Mr. Stompanato started shaking me and cursing me badly and saying, as he had told me before, no matter what I did nor how I tried to get away, he would never let me."

Lana Turner in an emotional testimony in front of a jury at the coroner's inquest.

station where she confessed to stabbing Stompanato in self-defense (a justifiable homicide). But the police booked her on suspicion of murder and took her to Juvenile Hall. The shocking and juicy story made headlines across the country. Most of the public and the press were sympathetic to Turner and Cheryl, except, of course, for Stompanato's gangster friends who wanted to see Cheryl punished.

There was never a trial. Instead, the case was decided at a coroner's inquest where, a week after the murder, the medical examiner in charge presided over a special court to decide on the cause of death. The inquest was broadcast live on TV and radio, but Cheryl didn't have to testify since the prosecutor said it would be too traumatic. Turner, however, gave what many considered the performance of her life on the stand. She spent an hour emotionally recalling the events leading up to the stabbing of Stompanato and describing them as heroic acts of self-defense. It took the jury less than 30 minutes to unanimously declare the murder a justifiable homicide. The prosecutor agreed and said he wouldn't pursue criminal charges against Cheryl.

WHY WE STILL CARE

☆ **This scandal put a spotlight on domestic abuse in Hollywood, and the US.** During the 1950s, domestic violence (when one member of a couple physically harms another) was considered a private matter and police rarely got involved. This is probably why Cheryl was

THE AFTERMATH

Cheryl Crane: After being cleared of the murder charges, Cheryl was placed in her grandmother's care for two years. She was then sent to El Retiro, an expensive home outside LA for troubled girls, and was officially released after her 18th birthday. She and model Jocelyn "Josh" LeRoy exchanged vows in a commitment ceremony in 1992. The couple still lives together in Palm Springs, California, where Cheryl is a real estate agent and a gay rights advocate.

Lana Turner: The bombshell actress continued her successful acting career and married three more times for a grand total of seven husbands and eight marriages (she married Cheryl's father twice). She (probably wisely) spent the last 23 years of her life single and died in 1995 at the age of 75.

pushed to such extreme measures. It's only in recent decades that domestic violence has begun to be taken seriously as a crime, starting with the Violence Against Women Act passed in 1994, which imposed heftier penalties for domestic violence and tripled federal funding for battered women's shelters.

Turner perfected the art of spinning a scandal. After Cheryl murdered Stompanato but *before* anyone called the police, Turner called her mother and her lawyer to start the damage control before the press could get hold of the story. Knowing the story would be all over the papers, they wanted to make sure it would be their take on the murder—an innocent child protecting her abused mother from a violent gangster—that made it into print. Turner's emotional defense of her daughter at the coroner's inquest is still considered one of her greatest performances, and it worked. Cheryl was found not guilty.

MORE HOLLYWOOD DOMESTIC DISPUTES

➡️ *Ike and Tina Turner.* The Grammy-winning R&B and soul couple rose to superstardom in the 1960s and '70s, but (as she wrote about in her autobiography, *I, Tina*) Ike was addicted to drugs and had a bad habit of hitting her. She escaped the abusive relationship in 1975 and went on to become an even bigger star on her own. Ike, on the other hand, was arrested in 1989 for cocaine possession and missed his own induction into the Rock 'n' Roll Hall of Fame because he was stuck in jail.

➡️ *Phil and Brynn Hartman.* Brynn ended her rocky marriage to Saturday Night Live comedian Phil in 1998 by shooting and killing him in their bedroom. When police arrived hours later, she turned the gun on herself. Investigations into the murder-suicide revealed Brynn's history of substance abuse and her violent possessiveness—a deadly combination that led to the tragic deaths.

➡️ *Rihanna and Chris Brown.* Hip hop hotties Brown and Rihanna seemed like the perfect pair—until news broke in February of 2009 that Brown had turned himself in to police after "a woman" accused him of violently attacking her. Police pictures of a battered and bruised Rihanna were then leaked to gossip site TMZ.com making even bigger headlines. The couple broke up, and Brown agreed to a plea deal that involved five years probation, 180 days of community service, and a mandatory yearlong domestic abuse counseling program.

THE SCOOP!

In the 1950s, TV quiz shows were so popular that almost every winning contestant became a minor celebrity. But viewers felt betrayed when they learned that the shows were being fixed.

WHAT WENT DOWN

When the very first TV quiz show, *The $64,000 Question*, premiered in June of 1955, it was an instant smash hit, winning over 47 million viewers after just two months. Each week, contestants would be asked a series of questions in a chosen category. They won money for every correct answer, and the money doubled as the questions became more difficult. Viewers loved cheering on their favorite contestants whom they hoped would score the $64,000 prize (which is equivalent to $500,000 today).

Soon, the studios were all rushing to put new shows on the air, including what became the

most famous quiz show, *Twenty-One*, in 1956. *Twenty-One* tested one's general knowledge, and questions were worth a certain number of points based on difficulty. But the questions were too hard for many, and sometimes contestants remained tied at zero, making the show so boring that its sponsor, Geritol, threatened to pull the plug within the first month.

To boost ratings, producer Dan Enright selected Charles Van Doren to be on the show. Van Doren was handsome, smart, and from a famous literary family. In his first show, he was pitted against *Twenty-One's* previous

THE PLAYERS

→ Daniel Enright
Crooked Producer

→ Charles Van Doren
Handsome Quiz Show Celebrity

→ Herbert Stempel
Whistle Blower #1

→ Ed Hilgemeyer
Whistle Blower #2

→ James Snodgrass
Whistle Blower #3

Contestants in their isolation booths
on the set of *Twenty-One*.

big winner contestant, Herb Stempel, and beat him in a showdown that was watched by an estimated 50 million viewers. During his three-month winning streak on *Twenty-One*, Van Doren won more than $100,000 and became the face of quiz show fame. *Time* magazine put him on its cover and dubbed him the "The Wizard of Quiz," and NBC offered him a lucrative contract as a commentator on the *Today Show*.

While Van Doren was busy basking in his newfound fame, a bitter Stempel started to tell people that *Twenty-One* was fixed: Favored contestants, he said, were fed answers by the producers, and the results of each competition were determined before it took place—all to bump up ratings for the show. At first, the public dismissed him as a sore loser, but, by 1958, more voices were joining the chorus. James Snodgrass, another *Twenty-One* contestant, also said he'd been on a fixed show. And it wasn't

QUOTEABLES

"I would give almost anything I have to reverse the course of my life in the last three years. I cannot take back one word or action; the past does not change for anyone. But at least I can learn from the past."

Charles Van Doren, in his emotional testimony before the House Committee, admitting to taking part in the fraud.

"A degree of deception is of considerable value in producing shows."

Part of *Twenty-One* producer Dan Enright's very honest testimony before the House.

just *Twenty-One*. Ed Hilgemeyer, a stand-by contestant on the quiz show *Dotto*, went public with a notebook he found backstage that was filled with all the answers the winning contestant had just given on air.

Accusations and evidence piled up against various quiz shows, and, in 1959, the case went before congress. The congressional hearings made front-page news as ex-quiz-show players (including Stempel and Hilgemeyer) testified about the fraud. But the most anticipated testimony came from Van Doren, who'd continuously maintained his innocence. Putting the last nail in the quiz industry's coffin, he shocked the nation by breaking down and revealing the truth: that he took part in the fraud, too.

THE AFTERMATH

Charles Van Doren: After the hearings, Van Doren became hugely unpopular. *Time*, the magazine that put him on its cover just two years before, described his testimony as full of "pomposity, self-pity and self-dramatization." He was fired from the *Today Show* and from Columbia University where he was a professor. He eventually went on to become an editor for the Encyclopedia Britannica, wrote several books, and is now an adjunct professor at the University of Connecticut. Van Doren rarely speaks out about the scandal and refused a $100,000 offer to be a consultant on the 1994 film version of the scandal, *Quiz Show*.

Herb Stempel: In 1960, Stempel was denied readmittance to New York University where he was completing his doctorate. He later taught public school and worked as a researcher for the New York City Department of Transportation. Unlike Van Doren, when the producers of *Quiz Show* offered him $30,000 to consult on the movie, he welcomed the opportunity.

TV Quiz Shows: After the hearings, all of the quiz show creators and producers who had been involved in the scandal were blackballed from working in TV. Since what they did wasn't illegal at the time, no charges could be pressed, but in 1960 congress did pass a law banning the fixing of quiz shows. The public quickly lost interest in quiz shows, and they disappeared from the air. Then, in the 1970s, similar shows like *Jeopardy, Wheel of Fortune*, and *Who Wants to Be a Millionaire* started to resurface. But networks were careful to call them "game shows" instead of quiz shows and put limits on how many times or how much money a contestant could win.

WHY WE STILL CARE

☆ **Quiz shows are early examples of reality TV.** Like 1950s quiz shows, current reality TV shows are advertised as real human drama, but behind the scenes most are (at least partially) scripted to create exciting story lines that keep viewers tuned in. Charles Van Doren, Herbert Stempel, and the rest of the quiz show winners were really the first reality TV stars, handpicked and groomed by the producers, and given the chance to become famous on TV for playing themselves.

☆ **The scandal changed how TV shows are paid for.** Like most early TV shows, quiz shows had single sponsorships. Each show was paid for by one company, and only that company's product was advertised during the show. This is why *Twenty-One*'s sponsor, Geritol, had so much influence over whether or not it stayed on the air. After the quiz show scandal, TV networks started airing commercials from multiple advertisers throughout shows. This way, advertisers have less financial risk (they pay less to show one commercial than to sponsor an entire show), and they have less control over whether a show gets pulled.

MORE ATTEMPTS TO BOOST RATINGS IN THE '50s

➡ **Color TV.** The sitcom *Beulah* set out to break color barriers when ABC released it in 1950 as the first show on television to star an African American. The show wasn't without controversy, though. Many in the black community saw the lead character, Beulah, who was a maid for a white family, as a derogatory portrayal of African Americans.

➡ **Monkey in the Morning.** When the *Today Show* was looking for a ratings boost after their first year on air, in 1952, it added a new co-host: a baby chimp. From 1953 to 1957, the chimp, J. Fred Muggs, played the piano, pretended to read the newspaper, bit his co-host Martha Raye, and raised the ratings through the roof.

➡ **Lucy's Baby.** Real-life couple Lucy and Desi Arnaz played a married couple on the hit sitcom *I Love Lucy*. But when Lucy became pregnant in real life in 1952, the couple was worried its audience would be scandalized by seeing proof that they actually had sex (sounds odd today, but shows were conservative back then and Lucy and Desi slept in separate beds on the show). Producers, however, allowed Lucy (the character) to also be pregnant and even had an episode (nine months later) in which Lucy gave birth on TV. Forty-four million viewers tuned in.

THE SCOOP!

Harvard psychology professors Timothy Leary and Richard Alpert were kicked out of the university after conducting experiments of hallucinogenic drugs on students, but not before they became the decade's psychedelic heroes.

WHAT WENT DOWN

At first, Timothy Leary seemed like your average academic. He got a PhD in psychology from the University of California Berkeley, wrote a well-respected book called *The Interpersonal Diagnosis of Personality*, and lectured at Harvard.

Then, after a year at Harvard, Leary read an article in *Life* magazine about a place in Mexico where shamans (holy people) were using "magic" mushrooms to alter consciousness and induce states that made people feel closer to God. The "magic" mushrooms naturally contained the chemical psilocybin, which causes hallucinogenic effects like euphoria and life-changing spiritual awakenings in people who ingest it. Leary traveled to Mexico to try the mushrooms.

THE PLAYERS

→ Timothy Leary
Radical Harvard
Professor #1

→ Richard Alpert
(a.k.a. Ram Dass)
Radical Harvard
Professor #2

Leary's experience on the mushrooms (also knows as a "trip") was so profound that he wanted to study the use of hallucinogens whe he returned to Harvard. He believed that taking psilocybin (and other hallucinogenic drugs, like the synthetic LSD, which had similar effects) could expand and heal the mind. A the time, these hallucinogens were legal in the US and easy to get for research studies. Leary teamed up with fellow Harvard psychology professor Richard Alpert, and the pair created the Harvard Psilocybin Project: a series of experiments designed to investigate the psychological benefits of psilocybin.

As part of the study, Leary and Alpert gave psilocybin to inmates who were about to be paroled at a nearby prison to see if it could keep them from committing new crimes and returning to jail and to divinity students to see if it would give them profound religious experiences. They also gave psilocybin to volunteer students to see, well, just to see what would happen.

The study went on for two years, and, by 1962, the drug-pushing duo's research started to raise some eyebrows on the Harvard campus because of how the research was being conducted. Test subjects were never warned that they could have a bad experience (i.e., hours of terrifying hallucinations and paranoia) when they took the psilocybin. Plus, Leary, Alpert, and their fellow researchers started taking hallucinogens along with their subjects in environments that looked a lot more like house parties than legit laboratory settings.

Timothy Leary in 1966.

QUOTEABLES

"I gave way to delight as mystics have for centuries when they peeked through the curtains and discovered that this world—so manifestly real—was actually a tiny stage set constructed by the mind."

Timothy Leary in his 1983 autobiography, *Flashbacks*, describing his first trip on psilocybin, which took place in Mexico.

"Tune in, turn on, drop out."

Timothy Leary's famous tagline, which became the catch phrase of the 1960s counterculture revolution.

Under fire from Harvard, Alpert and Leary reluctantly agreed to follow a set of rules imposed by the school, like having a physician present while subjects were being given psilocybin and promising not to use undergrads as test subjects. But Leary and Alpert were both soon fired anyway. Leary had stopped showing up for his classes and Alpert was caught giving psilocybin to undergrads. Their dismissals brought more attention to their project, and soon everyone knew about hallucinogenic drugs. In 1966, psilocybin and LSD became illegal in the US, but scholars say more than one million people had already taken them.

THE AFTERMATH

The Research Project: Leary and Alpert first took their project to Mexico (but got deported) and then to a 63-room mansion in Millbrook, New York. They called it research, but it was more like a drug commune with guest appearances by famous writers and an occasional police raid. The party lasted five years, during which Leary, Alpert, and another hallucinogenic enthusiast, Ralph Metzner, wrote a bestselling book called *The Psychedelic Experience*.

Timothy Leary: Leary remained a driving force of the '60s counterculture until 1970, when he was sentenced to 10 years in a California prison for marijuana possession. He escaped from prison and fled to Algeria where he lived with fugitive members of the Black Panthers, a radical black power movement. Leary was eventually caught in 1973 and returned to prison but was then pardoned by California Governor Jerry Brown in 1976. He spent the rest of his life giving speeches at college campuses and wrote more than 30 books. He also started a small software company, designed computer games, and was an early proponent of the wonders of the internet. He died from prostate cancer in 1996, but not before his last radical move: broadcasting his final weeks live on the internet and having some of his cremated remains launched into space.

Richard Alpert: Alpert became interested in drugless ways to reach higher states of consciousness. In 1967, he traveled to India where he met his spiritual guru, Neem Karoli Baba, who taught him about meditation and spiritual practice, and gave him the name Ram Dass. In 1971, Ram Dass published his famous spiritual book *Be Here Now*. Since then, he's been involved in a number of worthy causes. In 1997, he suffered from a stroke that left him partially paralyzed and unable to travel. He now teaches nationally via podcast and from his home in Maui.

WHY WE STILL CARE

★ **Timothy Leary helped shape the counterculture movement of the 1960s.** Because of Leary's experiments, young people everywhere started trying hallucinogens to achieve altered states of consciousness. Bands named themselves after drugs and wrote music about doing drugs, while artists created psychedelic art that mimicked what the world looked like on hallucinogens. Though hallucinogenic drugs aren't as popular as they were in the 1960s and are now illegal, they are still popular among college students, artists, and spiritual seekers.

★ **The Harvard Psilocybin Project halted further research on mind-altering drugs.** The federal government made psilocybin and LSD illegal in 1966 and halted research on the therapeutic and medical benefits of drugs like psilocybin, LSD, marijuana, and MDMA (the club drug ecstasy) for the next 30 years. Research into these drugs has only recently started up again. Medicinal marijuana has since become legal in many states, and both MDMA and psilocybin are now being tested to treat various psychological disorders.

MORE PSYCHEDELIC PIONEERS

➡ **Aldous Huxley.** Huxley's 1954 book, *The Doors of Perception* (which the band The Doors got their name from), documented one long trip on the hallucinogen mescaline. Huxley concluded that psychedelic experiences would make you a better person, and *The Doors of Perception* became a bible for those looking to attain deeper states of consciousness, including Leary and Alpert.

➡ **Ken Kesey.** While Kesey is famous for writing the book *One Flew Over the Cuckoo's Nest*, he's more famous for heading the Merry Pranksters, a group of far-out travelers who crossed the country on LSD in 1964 in a day-glo-painted bus they called "Further." After the trip, Kesey moved to La Honda, California, where he threw strobe-lit acid parties and became the main character in Tom Wolfe's book *The Electric Kool-Aid Acid Test*.

➡ **Augustus Owsley Stanley III.** More commonly known as "Bear," Stanley was the chemist behind the most popular LSD in the 1960s, making and distributing over a million doses of the drug between 1965 and 1967. The word "owsley" is even in the Oxford Dictionary as a slang term for really good LSD. Stanley also briefly managed the band The Grateful Dead, who thanked him by referencing him in their lyrics.

BLACK ATHLETES STAGE CONTROVERSIAL PROTEST AT OLYMPICS

1968

THE SCOOP!

After winning Olympic medals in the 200-meter race at the Mexico City Olympics in 1968, African American runners Tommie Smith and John Carlos sparked a controversy that got them thrown out of the games and became a huge event in civil rights history.

WHAT WENT DOWN

It was the summer of 1968 and the civil rights movement was at its height. Martin Luther King, Jr. had been assassinated a few months earlier and people were staging protests all over the country, demanding equal rights for African Americans. A year before, Harry Edwards, a prominent black sociology professor, formed the Olympic Project for Human Rights (OPHR) to protest racial segregation in the US, especially in sports.

The OPHR originally advocated for black athletes to boycott the 1968 Olympics until the organization's demands for an end to racial segregation were met. Though the boycott was called off, Edwards urged Olympic athletes, including Tommie Smith and John Carlos, to protest in smaller ways at the Olympics.

At the Olympics that year, Smith won the gold and Carlos won the bronze in the 200-meter race. When they arrived on the podium to accept their medals, they were both shoeless and wore black socks, OPHR badges, and

THE PLAYERS

➡ Tommie Smith
Gold Medal Winner

➡ John Carlos
Bronze Medal Winner

➡ Harry Edwards
Activist Sociologist

➡ Avery Brundage
President of the
International Olympic
Committee

Tommie Smith and John Carlos giving the black power salute at the 1968 Olympics.

one black glove each. When the "Star Spangled Banner" played, they shocked the viewing public and the International Olympic Committee (IOC) by bowing their heads and raising their gloved fists in the "Black Power" salute. The salute was meant to be a symbol of black pride. But since the salute was widely used by The Black Panthers, a radical African American group that challenged the power held by white Americans, the mostly white audience considered the salute unpatriotic. Smith and Carlos later explained in interviews that the black socks represented black poverty in a racist US, and the salute itself was a protest against the continuing discrimination that blacks endured.

QUOTEABLES

"If I win I am an American, not a black American. But if I did something bad then they would say 'a Negro.' We are black and we are proud of being black."

Tommie Smith, explaining his position at a press conference after the medals ceremony.

"[This protest is] a deliberate and violent breach of the fundamental principles of the Olympic spirit."

A statement released by the IOC in the aftermath of the protest.

Avery Brundage, president of the IOC, was outraged by the protest, saying that the athletes' actions went against the historically apolitical environment at the Olympics. He demanded Smith and Carlos be thrown off the US Olympic team and taken out of the games. The US team initially tried to defend the men but faced too much pressure from the IOC and sent both athletes home to an unwelcoming American public.

WHY WE STILL CARE

☆ **The scandal reminds us of the racist climate of the '60s.** Though Smith and Carlos were simply trying to bring attention to the lack of civil rights for African Americans, the mostly white country saw the protest as offensive and unpatriotic, and felt that the athletes should have been grateful to simply be in the Olympics.

THE AFTERMATH

John Carlos: After the Olympics, Carlos had a difficult time rehabilitating his image and fell on hard times. He lost his first wife to suicide, which he believed was a result of the pressure put on the couple by negative press. As time passed, public opinion of the two activists changed, and Carlos became a liaison to the black community for the 1984 Olympic Committee.

Tommie Smith: Like Carlos, Smith's post-Olympic life was plagued by difficulties.

He'd been in the Army but was discharged from service for "Un-American activities" after the Olympic event (which, on the upside, kept him out of Vietnam). He later became a teacher, coach, and motivational speaker.

Carlos and Smith: Both men went on to become role models. In 2005, a statue celebrating their clenched fist salute was erected at San Jose State University (where they had gone to school), and in 2008 they were both awarded the Arthur Ashe Courage Award from ESPN.

MORE POLITICAL MOMENTS
AT THE OLYMPICS

➡️**Women are Permitted to Play.** The first modern Olympics were held in Greece in 1896, and only men were allowed to compete. In protest, a female Greek runner, Stamata Revithi, ran the 26-mile course for the marathon the day after the official race was run. Though she wasn't allowed into the stadium to cross the official finish line, she proved that women were tough enough for the Olympics, and they were included in the 1900 games.

➡️**British Royalty Gets Dissed.** At the 1908 games in London, the American team refused to "dip" their flag to British royals as they passed by during the opening ceremony. The dip was a symbol of respect. By refusing to do it, Americans were taking a stand against their former colonizers and showing solidarity with Irish athletes who were still under Great Britain's rule. Many athletes on the American team, including the flag bearer, were either Irish immigrants or descendants of Irish immigrants.

➡️**The US Plays with Hitler.** Many Americans urged a US boycott of the 1936 Olympic games held in Berlin while Hitler was chancellor. (It was before World War II, but Hitler was already considered a tyrant.) Avery Brundage, President of the American Olympic Committee and the same Brundage who had Smith and Carlos thrown out of the 1968 Olympics, convinced the American team to participate.

➡️**An Olympic Cold War Begins.** The US, along with 60 other countries, boycotted the 1980 Olympics in Moscow to protest the Soviet Union's invasion of Afghanistan. In response, the Soviet Union boycotted the 1984 Olympics in Los Angeles.

THE SCOOP!

Presidential hopeful and Senator Ted Kennedy crashed his car in a tragic and mysterious incident that killed 28-year-old Mary Jo Kopechne and left the country wondering what really went on that night in Chappaquiddick.

WHAT WENT DOWN

In 1969, Ted Kennedy was a second-term Senator from Massachusetts, the youngest and only surviving brother in the politically powerful Kennedy family, that also seemed to be cursed with bad luck. (Two of Ted's brothers had been assassinated; Robert was killed the year before while campaigning for president, and John was killed in 1963 during his first presidential term.) Ted, 37, was thought to be a shoe-in as the Democratic presidential nominee in 1972 and maybe even the White House. On July 18, he attended a small party on Chappaquiddick—a little island in Martha's Vineyard, off the coast of Massachusetts. The party was a reunion thrown by the young female members of his late brother Robert's presidential campaign staff. Ted went to the party alone. His wife, Joan, who was pregnant at the time, stayed home.

THE PLAYERS

→ Ted Kennedy
Senator From Massachusetts

→ Mary Jo Kopechne
Politial Aide

According to later police reports, Ted claimed he left the party at around 11:15 pm with Mary Jo Kopechne, his late brother's political aide, stating that they were catching the last ferry back to Martha's Vineyard where they both had hotel reservations. The next morning the Oldsmobile they had driven in was found upside down in Poucha Pond (on the opposite side of the island from the ferry) with Kopechne's dead body inside.

Kennedy showed up at the local police station with his lawyers to report the accident 10 hours after it happened. He reported that on the way to the ferry, he took a wrong turn and ended up on a dirt road headed for Dike Bridge. He said he was unfamiliar with the road and driving too fast, and had accidentally driven off the bridge and into Poucha Pond. Kennedy said he was able to free himself from the car and swim to the surface, but he couldn't free Kopechne. He then said he walked the mile and a half back to the party and asked two male guests to drive him back to the pond. The men tried (unsuccessfully) to free Kopechne. After giving up hope, they drove to the ferry landing where Kennedy claims he jumped in the channel, swam the 527 feet to the other side, and walked the two blocks to his hotel where he went to sleep. His excuse for not reporting the accident earlier was that he was confused and lacked the "moral strength" needed to deal with the situation that night. But after he woke up (and called his lawyer) he went straight to the

The bridge Ted Kennedy drove off with Mary Jo Kopechne.

QUOTEABLES

"... I made immediate and repeated efforts to save Mary Jo by diving into strong and murky current, but succeeded only in increasing my state of utter exhaustion and alarm. My conduct and conversations during the next several hours, to the extent that I can remember them, make no sense to me at all ..."

Ted Kennedy in the nationally televised speech he made the day he pled guilty to leaving the scene of an accident, explaining his actions that night.

"It is my understanding that he [Kennedy] has already been, and will continue to be, punished far beyond anything this court can impose."

Judge James Boyle in a statement during Ted Kennedy's sentencing for leaving the scene of a crime, explaining why he was suspending the two-month prison sentence that would have been Kennedy's only punishment.

police. Kennedy was allowed to leave the station shortly after giving his statement.

The story was front-page news, and it didn't take long for people to notice that Kennedy's story didn't add up. Kopechne left her purse and hotel key at the party, which was odd if she really was going back to her hotel. It also seemed weird that Kennedy would make a wrong turn and get lost when he had driven to the ferry three times that day, and on the dirt road to Dike Bridge twice. Plus, a sheriff's deputy claimed he saw the couple in a car that looked like Kennedy's stopped by the turn to Dike Bridge an hour and a half after Kennedy claimed the accident happened, and when he got out of his car to see if they were okay, the car took off down the road toward the bridge. To many critics, it looked more like Kennedy and Kopechne had a few drinks and went on a joy ride looking for a secluded spot to get romantic.

Six days later, at a hearing in Martha's Vineyard, Kennedy pled guilty to leaving the scene of an accident. His driver's license was suspended for a year, and he was sentenced the minimum, two-month, jail time. But the judge suspended the sentence, so he never went to jail. That night, Kennedy appeared on live national TV to ask for the public's forgiveness, but his speech was not well received.

The police investigation also indicated that Kopechne propably survived for hours in the submerged car thanks to an air pocket, but suffocated to death when the air ran out. So, if Kennedy had called the police right away,

THE AFTERMATH

Ted Kennedy: Massachusetts eventually forgave their beloved Senator and reelected him in 1970. But the scandal surrounding the accident forced him to scrap his plans to run for President in 1972 and 1976. When he finally did run in the Democratic primaries in 1979, an ABC News poll showed that 36 percent of Americans still held the accident against him and weren't planning to vote for him because of it. He lost the nomination to incumbent president Jimmy Carter. Kennedy remained a Massachusetts Senator for 46 years until his death in 2009 from brain cancer.

Mary Jo Kopechne: A funeral was held for Kopechne at St. Vincent's Church in Plymouth, Pennsylvania, three days after the accident in Chappaquiddick. Both Ted Kennedy and his pregnant wife (who suffered a miscarriage shortly after) attended the service. Kopechne's parents were later paid $140,923 by Kennedy's car insurance provider.

a rescue might have been possible. District Attorney Edmund Dinis wanted to charge Kennedy with manslaughter, but Kennedy's attorneys were diligent in ensuring that new evidence was never introduced. In the end, Kennedy was completely let off the hook.

WHY WE STILL CARE

☆ **The events leading to the death of Mary Jo Kopechne are still a mystery.** Because no autopsy was performed on Kopechne's body and because there were no further legal investigations into the holes in Kennedy's story, no one really knows what happened that night in Chappaquiddick. And perhaps no one ever will.

☆ **The scandal emphasized that money and power can buy freedom.** No matter what actually happened in Chappaquiddick, most people think Kennedy got off easy. None of the people involved ever spoke publicly about that night, Kopechne's family never sued for wrongful death in a civil trial, and though the inquest (a judicial investigation into the case) found that Kennedy probably lied about where he was going and what happened, no criminal charges were ever brought against him.

MORE VICTIMS OF THE KENNEDY CURSE

➡ **Joseph Kennedy, Jr.** (the eldest of nine Kennedy kids) was killed during a risky World War II mission in 1944. He was 29.

➡ **Kathleen Kennedy** (kid number four) was killed in a plane crash in France in 1948. She was 28.

➡ **President John F. Kennedy** (kid number two) was assassinated in a presidential motorcade in 1963, three years into his presidency. He was 46.

➡ **Robert Kennedy** (kid number seven), a former Attorney General and New York Senator, was assassinated in 1968 after winning the Democratic presidential primary in California. He was 42.

➡ **David Kennedy**, one of Robert's children, died of a drug overdose in 1984 in a Palm Beach, Florida, hotel room. He was 28.

➡ **Michael Kennedy**, another one of Robert's children, died when he accidentally skied into a tree in Aspen in 1997. He was 39.

➡ **John F. Kennedy, Jr.**, President Kennedy's only son, died along with his wife and sister-in-law in a tragic plane crash near Martha's Vineyard in 1999. He was 38.

THE SCOOP!

The US National Guard killed four college students and injured nine during an antiwar protest at Kent State University.

WHAT WENT DOWN

When Richard Nixon ran for president, he promised that he was going to pull the US out of the war in Vietnam. The country had been involved for nearly six years, more than 30,000 American soldiers had already died, and no one was really even sure why we were there. But less than two years later, on April 30, 1970, President Nixon went on national TV to announce that American troops were being sent to invade Cambodia, a country we weren't even fighting with, in order to "promote peace" in the region. It looked a lot like Nixon was expanding the war, not ending it.

THE PLAYERS

➡Richard Nixon
US President and Protest Instigator

➡James Rhodes
Governor of Ohio

➡Allison Krause, Sandra Lee Scheuer, Jeffrey Glenn Miller, and William K. Schroeder
Slain College Students

Many Americans were angry, especially college students. After all, they were the ones doing most of the fighting (the military draft affected men between the ages of 18 and 26). Soon, there were antiwar protests at college campuses all over the country. At Kent State University, just outside Cleveland, Ohio, students rioted in front of downtown bars, broke store windows, and started fires. Late that night, the mayor of Kent set a curfew for the town and campus, declared a state of emergency in Kent, and asked Ohio Governor James

The armed National Guard at Kent State University.

Rhodes to call in the National Guard to control the campus.

The next day, protestors set fire to an old and abandoned Army ROTC building on campus to protest the National Guard's presence on campus. When firefighters attempted to put the flames out, protesters threw rocks at them and slashed their hoses. On the third day, Governor Rhodes declared a state of emergency at Kent State, banned all protests, and gave the National Guard the go-ahead to use force and weapons like tear gas and bayonets to control the crowds—and they did.

QUOTEABLES

"We take these actions, not for the purpose of expanding the war into Cambodia, but for the purpose of ending the war in Vietnam, and winning the just peace we all desire."

President Richard Nixon announcing the invasion into Cambodia that sparked the protests.

"[These protestors are] worse than the brown shirts and the communist element ... they're the worst type of people that we harbor in America, and I want to say that they're not going to take over campus!"

Part of the inflammatory speech Ohio Governor James Rhodes gave at a press conference in Kent on the third day of protests in May of 1970.

On the fourth day of protests, approximately 1,500 students gathered on the campus commons and the surrounding hills to protest. Classes were letting out and more students gathered around to see what was going on. The guardsmen ordered everyone to clear the area and fired tear gas on the crowd in case they still didn't get the hint. Students started to disperse and the guardsmen started to retreat.

Then, unexpectedly, a group of 28 guardsmen turned back around and started shooting into the crowd. More than 60 shots were fired in just 13 seconds. Four students were killed, and nine were wounded, including one student who was permanently paralyzed. Ironically, none of the victims had been involved in the downtown riots or the burning of the ROTC building—they were just onlookers. Four of them were shot from behind.

Kent State University was immediately shut down, all students and faculty were evacuated from the school, and all of the businesses and streets leading to the downtown Kent area surrounding the campus were closed. The campus remained closed for the rest of the semester, but graduating seniors were allowed to have their commencement ceremony in June where 1,250 students graduated.

THE AFTERMATH

The Shootings: The shootings sparked countrywide student protests. Outraged students at 441 US colleges shut down their schools, occupied buildings, and boycotted classes to protest the murders of their fellow students in Ohio.

The National Guard: Some of the 28 guardsmen claimed they started shooting because they were outnumbered and felt threatened. Others claimed that a sniper fired at them first. The President's Commission on Campus Unrest described the use of firepower as "unnecessary, unwarranted, and inexcusable." But the report also said that the students' violent behavior played a big part in the tragedy. In 1974, federal charges were filed against eight of the guardsmen, but the charges were dropped due to a lack of evidence, and the guardsmen were never punished.

The Students: The surviving victims and the families of the slain students filed a civil case against the state of Ohio, and after five years of legal wrangling they eventually settled out of court for $675,000, which was split between the 13 families.

☆ **The Kent State shootings showed how big the divide was between older and younger generations.** The older, more conservative Americans saw the protesters as a dangerous element to be dealt with, and younger more liberal Americans thought their voices were being violently silenced.

☆ **Real bullets are no longer used for crowd control.** Police and national guardsmen may still be called in to break up protests, but after the Kent State shootings live ammunition was replaced with rubber bullets, bean bags, pepper spray, and noise cannons—all of which are now typically used at protests to more peacefully disperse crowds.

MORE HISTORICAL POLITICAL PROTESTS

➡ ***Maori Moon.*** In the New Zealand Maori culture, *whakapohane* (directing your bare butt at a hated target) is considered the worst possible insult. So when Prince Charles and Lady Di came to visit New Zealand in 1983, Maori land rights activist Dun Mihaka, who was protesting the loss of Maori land to British settlers back in the 1800s, mooned the British royalty.

➡ ***Tree Sitting.*** Eco-activist Julia "Butterfly" Hill spent 738 days living on a small wooden platform perched on the branches of a 1,000-year-old redwood tree to keep the Pacific Lumber Company from chopping it down. Hill's supporters used a pulley system to deliver food and supplies, and eco-loving celebrities like Joan Baez and Woody Harrelson climbed 180 feet to visit her in her new home. The lumber company eventually gave in and agreed to spare the tree—along with other trees within a three-acre radius—if Hill would just come down already.

➡ ***Shoe Attack.*** At a 2008 press conference with the Iraqi Prime Minister in Baghdad, an Iraqi journalist let George W. Bush know exactly what he thought about the President's foreign policy by chucking his shoes at Bush's head. In Middle Eastern culture, throwing a shoe at someone is a huge sign of disrespect (and it can really hurt). However, Bush managed to duck in time and escaped unharmed.

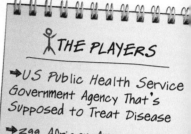

THE SCOOP!

For 40 years, the US Public Health Service let African Americans die of syphilis (a disease they could have cured) so they could study its effects. When a news article about the study was finally publicized in 1972, it became the worst example of racism and unethical behavior in US medical history.

WHAT WENT DOWN

In the 1920s, syphilis (a sexually transmitted disease) was a big problem in the South, especially in poor African American communities. It's a highly contagious disease that can cause painful rashes and sores, as well as damage to the internal organs, insanity, and even death. At the time, it was incurable. The US Public Health Service (PHS) planned to start a program to treat it, but when the Great Depression hit in 1929, the PHS no

longer had the money to fund treatments. Then, a PHS doctor had an idea to switch things up and study the long-term effects of *untreated* syphilis instead. The idea was to find people with the disease, monitor them until they died, and then perform autopsies on their bodies to better understand what syphilis can do to the human body. They reasoned that poor, uneducated African-American men would be good candidates for the highly unethical study.

The PHS teamed up with the Tuskegee Institute (a well-known African American university) on a new study called "The Tuskegee Study of Untreated Syphilis in the Negro Male." Together they recruited 399 African-American men with syphilis from the Macon

⚕ THE PLAYERS

→ US Public Health Service
Government Agency That's
Supposed to Treat Disease

→ 399 African American Men
Unsuspecting Victims

A researcher with participants in the Tuskegee Syphilis Study.

County, Alabama, area. The men who signed up for the study were told they had "bad blood" (local slang that described several illnesses, including syphilis, anemia, and fatigue). They were never told they had syphilis specifically, but were told they'd be given free treatment for the bad blood, along with meals, burial insurance, and medical exams. But in truth, they didn't receive any medical treatment.

In the 1930s, syphilis treatment wasn't terribly advanced, so the untreated men in the study weren't missing out on much for the first 10 years of the study. (Though they *were* being lied to.) But by the 1940s, the disease was being safely treated and cured with penicillin. *Still*, the study's doctors chose

QUOTEABLES

"Men who were poor and African American, without resources and with few alternatives, they believed they had found hope when they were offered free medical care by the United States Public Health Service. They were betrayed ... Our government is supposed to protect the rights of it's citizens; their rights were trampled on.

President Bill Clinton in May of 1997 in an official apology for the Tuskegee Syphilis Study.

"The study began when attitudes were much different on treatment and experimentation. At this point in time, with our current knowledge of treatment and the disease and the revolutionary change in approach to human experimentation, I don't believe the program would be undertaken."

Dr. J. D. Millar, who was in charge of the Tuskegee Syphilis Study in 1972, defending the study in the bombshell *New York Times* article.

not to treat the men, to keep the experiment going. To make matters worse, the doctors also ensured that the participants didn't receive treatment for or information about syphilis from local physicians throughout the 40 years (1932–1972) that the Tuskegee Syphilis study took place. This meant that the men not only got sicker and sicker, but that they unknowingly passed on the disease through sex with their girlfriends and wives, who then passed it on during pregnancy to any children they had after being infected.

In 1972, a reporter from the Associated Press found out about the study and released a bombshell article about it that made the front page of the *New York Times*. Many people in the medical community already knew about the study, but they convinced themselves it was important for the greater health of the public. Once the American public heard about it, though, people were horrified. The government immediately appointed an advisory panel to review the study, and the panel did not like what it found: The study participants were clueless about what they had signed up for, denied treatment for an easily treatable disease, and allowed to die. The panel declared the study "ethically un-justified" and advised putting a stop to it at once. The study was shut down in October of 1972, though only 74 of the 399 participants with syphilis lived to learn the truth.

THE AFTERMATH

The Victims: A class action lawsuit was filed on behalf of the study's participants and their families in 1973. A year later, the US government settled with the families out of court for $10 million dollars, lifetime medical benefits, and burial services for all the living participants. The wives and children of the participants were guaranteed the same benefits a couple of years later. The last study survivor died in 2004.

The Study: In 1996, The Tuskegee Syphilis Study Legacy Committee demanded an official apology for the study from President Clinton on behalf of the government. The President released an official apology to the surviving study participants, their families, and the African American community at large on behalf of the government in 1997. He also established a $200,000 grant to create what is now the National Center of Bioethics at Tuskegee University.

⭐ **The Tuskegee Study changed the way medical research is conducted.** To make sure that the unethical and racist practices of the study wouldn't be repeated, Congress passed the National Research Act in 1974. The law requires medical research study organizers to obtain "informed consent" from anyone taking part in a study. This means that all participants must be told what the study is about and what is going to be done to them *before* they agree to join. It also requires any government-funded study to undergo an ethical board evaluation.

⭐ **The unethical treatment led to public distrust in the medical field.** After the details of the Tuskegee Syphilis Study were revealed, fear of exploitation kept African Americans from participating in other studies, donating organs, vaccinating their children, and even getting preventive care. As a result, The Tuskegee Syphilis Legacy Committee (the same committee that demanded an apology from President Clinton in 1996) made it a mission to develop a strategy to address the damages of the Tuskegee Study and restore public trust.

MORE UNETHICAL STUDIES

➡ *Another Syphilis Study.* The same US Public Health Service (PHS) purposely infected hundreds in Guatemala with syphilis (without their knowledge) from 1946 to 1948 to test the effectiveness of penicillin in treating the disease. They used mainly soldiers, prisoners, and mental patients, some of whom were infected by prostitutes (provided by the PHS) who had syphilis. A college professor who was researching the Tuskegee Syphilis Study uncovered the Guatamala study in 2010.

➡ *Unethical Drug Trial.* Dr. Richard Borison and Bruce Diamond made more than $10 million from 1989 to 1996 by running clinical trials on experimental drugs created to treat schizophrenia, anxiety, depression, and Alzheimer's disease. They told trial participants they were conducting the trials for the Medical College of Georgia, but in reality, drug companies were paying them to do the research. In 1997, some former employees blew the whistle on the duo.

➡ *AIDS and HIV Research.* In the 1980s, drug treatments for AIDS were only for adults. Then, the National Institutes of Health funded a series of studies between 1988 and 2001 to test the effectiveness of experimental drugs on HIV-positive children. The studies led to life-saving therapies, but, in 2005, the Associated Press reported that the test subjects included hundreds of foster children who were given the experimental drugs without proper permission from a guardian. The shocking revelation prompted Congressional hearings and stronger oversight for studies using foster children.

THE SCOOP!

An early morning break-in at the Watergate Hotel in Washington, DC, revealed a conspiracy that resulted in shocking news stories in *The Washington Post*, televised Senate hearings, and the resignation of President Richard Nixon.

THE PLAYERS

➡ Richard Nixon
Crooked President

➡ Bob Woodward and Carl Bernstein
Scandal-Breaking Reporters

➡ Deep Throat
Secret FBI Informant

WHAT WENT DOWN

In June of 1972, there was a suspicious break-in at the Democratic National Committee (DNC) headquarters on the sixth floor of the Watergate office complex. Five robbers were caught at 2:30 am with bugging devices, cameras, lock picks, tear gas, and thousands of dollars in cash. The next day, word got out that one of the burglars, James McCord, was a former CIA agent and the director of security for Rupublican President Richard Nixon's reelection committee.

The entire incident was just way too suspicious. *Washington Post* reporters Bob Woodward and Carl Bernstein began to dig around for info about the break-in with the help of an anonymous FBI informant they called Deep Throat, who gave Woodward inside info during secret late-night meetings. With Deep Throat's help, the reporters investigated the case and released one story after another in *The Washington Pos* during the summer and fall of 1972. The storie revealed that money from Nixon's reelection committee was used to pay the Watergate robbers, and that the break-in was part of a huge campaign to sabotage the Democrats. Still, Nixon's political reputation remained intact; h denied any personal involvement in the robber

nd there was no evidence to prove otherwise. He was
eelected by a landslide in November.

Iowever, investigations into the burglaries continued. By
ebruary of 1973, the five robbers plus two high-ranking
nembers of Nixon's reelection committee were jailed for
onspiracy, wiretapping, and burglary in connection with
he Watergate break-in. The investigations were leading
loser and closer to the President. Then, Nixon went on
ve TV in April of 1973 to tell Americans that while he
vasn't involved in Watergate, he'd asked four high-level
overnment employees with suspected involvement to
esign, including White House counsel, John Dean.

he Senate Watergate Committee conducted hearings to
urther investigate the scandal, which were broadcast live
n TV. When Dean was called to the stand, his testimony
xposed a complex system of break-ins, spying, and
abotage (of which Watergate was just a tiny part) that
he Nixon administration used to take down its politial enemies. He also testified that he'd discussed ways to
over up Watergate with Nixon at least 35 times, starting
ight after the break-in. But the most damaging testimony

President Nixon declares his innocence
on TV in August 1973.

QUOTEABLES

"I'm not a crook."

President Richard Nixon reaffirms his innocence in a November 17, 1973, press conference.

"Our long national nightmare is over."

President Gerald Ford during a speech he gave after being sworn into office on August 9, 1974.

at the hearings came a month later when a former White House aide revealed that Nixon had been secretly recording all his conversations and telephone calls since 1971. The Senate and federal prosecutors wanted those tapes and demanded that Nixon hand them over. Nixon refused, saying his "executive privilege" as President gave him the constitutional right to keep anything he wanted to a secret.

To keep them secret, Nixon tried to fire anyone who was questioning him, but the firings made him look even shadier, and people started calling out for his impeachment. Nixon finally agreed to give up *some* of the tapes, but they seemed to have suspicious gaps of silence on them. In July of 1974, the Supreme Court unanimously ruled that he needed to hand over *all* of the tapes, and a few days later, the Senate approved articles of impeachment that would put Nixon on trial for obstruction of justice and could get him kicked out of office. One tape in particular proved that Nixon knew who was behind the Watergate break-in, that he was in charge of the cover-up from the start, and that he even ordered the FBI to stop its investigation. At that point, it was clear that Nixon had two choices: to resign or be impeached. He resigned in August of 1974 making him the first president in history to leave office (alive) before his term was up.

THE AFTERMATH

The Reporters: Bob Woodward's and Carl Bernstein's investigative reports on Watergate won *The Washington Post* a Pulitzer Prize in 1973. The pair wrote a tell-all book called *All the President's Men*, which was released in 1974. In 1976, the book was made into an award-winning movie with the same name starring Robert Redford and Dustin Hoffman as Woodward and Bernstein, respectively.

Richard Nixon: After Nixon's resignation, Vice President Gerald Ford was sworn in as his replacement. Ford pardoned Nixon for any crimes connected with Watergate, which meant that although more than 30 officials involved in the scandal served jail time, Nixon never would. In 1994, Nixon died of a stroke at the age of 81. More of his tapes were released after his death, and they revealed that he was involved in raising hush money to keep the Watergate burglars quiet and had been a part of dozens of other criminal activities.

Deep Throat: Deep Throat's identity remained a mystery until 2005, when Mark Felt, who had been the number two man at the FBI during the Watergate scandal, came out to the world in a *Vanity Fair* article.

☆ **Watergate made many Americans lose trust in the government.** Right after Nixon resigned, a Gallup poll showed that public trust in the Executive Branch of Government (headed by the President) plummeted from 73 percent to 40 percent, and it's never really recovered. As recently as 2008, the same poll showed trust at near-Watergate levels: 42 percent.

☆ **The scandal started a "–gate" trend.** Probably the most annoying and lasting effect of the Watergate scandal has been the press' obsession with using the suffix "–gate" in the name of every public scandal since 1973. When figure skater Nancy Kerrigan was attacked before a competition in 1994, the scandal was called Skategate (page 182). When it came out that White House intern Monica Lewinsky was having an affair with then President Clinton, it was called Monicagate (page 194). And when Justin Timberlake exposed Janet Jackson's bare boob at the Super Bowl in 2004, the incident became known as Nipplegate.

MORE NOT SO GREAT LEADERS

➡ *James Buchanan (1857 to 1861).* The country was divided over slavery while Democratic President Buchanan was in office, but he never took a stand on anything, including stopping the Civil War. He claimed he was against slavery, but he made compromises that spread the practice out West. Then, when the South said they were going to withdraw from the Union (marking the start of the Civil War), Buchanan said that, while he didn't think it was legal, there wasn't anything he could do to stop them.

➡ *Warren G. Harding (1921 to 1923).* This Republican President spent most of his time in office chasing women, playing golf, and passing any law Republicans in Congress wanted to implement. His cabinet was filled with corrupt cronies who took advantage of his inattention and got involved in all kinds of scams, like taking bribes from oilmen to drill on government land. Harding eventually realized what was going on in his cabinet but died of a heart attack before he could do anything about it.

➡ *Herbert Hoover (1929 to 1933).* Republican President Hoover was elected right before the stock market crash of 1929, which kicked off the Great Depression. He promised the people a speedy recovery from their monetary woes, but he didn't really have a good plan to fix things. He cut taxes and hired people for public works jobs, but ultimately thought that to boost the economy, Americans had to find ways to help themselves, which wasn't what Americans wanted to hear when they had lost their jobs, homes, and farms. He only made it through one term.

THE SCOOP!

In the beginning of 1974, Patty Hearst, granddaughter of famous newspaper magnate William Randolph Hearst, was just your average 19-year-old heiress—until she was kidnapped by the domestic terrorist group the Simbionese Liberation Army (SLA) and later put on trial for joining them.

WHAT WENT DOWN

In the 1970s, most people knew of Patty Hearst because she was from a wealthy, high-profile family. Her grandfather William Randolph Hearst was a powerful newspaper and magazine tycoon. She was a student at the University of California Berkeley in February of 1974 when three armed members of the Simbionese Liberation Army (SLA), a domestic terrorist group that opposed capitalism and American society in general, burst into her Berkeley apartment, beat up her fiancé, and stuffed her into the trunk of a car. Their original plan was to use Hearst to bargain for the release of two SLA members who were on trial for murder. When authorities refused, the SLA switched gears and demanded that the Hearst family distribute food to all the poor people in California. Hearst's dad, Randolph Hearst, spent millions of dollars distributing food throughout the state, but the SLA refused to release her.

THE PLAYERS

➡️ Patty Hearst
Abducted Heiress

➡️ William Randolph Hearst
Newspaper Magnate and Patty's Grandfather

➡️ Simbionese Liberation Army
Radical Leftist Abductors

➡️ F. Lee Bailey
High-Profile Lawyer

Patty Hearst posing in front of the SLA emblem in 1974.

Then, less than two months after Hearst's kidnapping, the SLA released a shocking recording to a local radio station. In it, Hearst called her parents "pigs," declared she'd joined the SLA, and announced that she'd changed her name to Tania (after Cuban Communist revolutionary Tania the Guerilla, girlfriend of rebel Che Gueverra). The shocking recording made many people wonder what was going on. Two weeks later, Hearst was captured on a security camera wielding a machine gun during the SLA's robbery of a Hibernia Bank in San Francisco. More than $10,000 was stolen and two bystanders were shot by other SLA members. After the robbery, Hearst turned from kidnap victim to wanted criminal. She was finally arrested (along with four other members of the SLA) in San Francisco almost a year later.

QUOTEABLES

"Death to the fascist insect that preys upon the life of the people."
The official slogan of the Simbionese Liberation Army (SLA).

"Greetings to the people, this is Tania. On April 15, my comrades and I expropriated $10,660.02 from the Sunset branch of Hibernia Bank. Casualties could have been avoided had the persons involved kept out of the way and cooperated with the people's forces until after our departure."
Patty Hearst in a recorded statement that was released by the SLA after the Hibernia Bank robbery.

When she was booked by police, Hearst listed her occupation as "urban guerrilla." It certainly looked like she'd willingly joined the SLA. But when her trial for the Hibernia Bank robbery began four months later, Hearst's famous defense lawyer, F. Lee Bailey, painted a very different picture. Bailey (with Hearst's testimony) argued that the only reason Hearst took part in the robbery was because she'd been brainwashed by her abductors, that she'd been physically and sexually abused, and kept blindfolded in a closet for almost two months until she agreed to join the SLA. Hearst also testified that she'd only taken part in the Hibernia Bank rob-

bery because she was afraid she'd be killed if she refused. Despite her defense, Hearst was found guilty of armed bank robbery and sentenced to seven years in jail.

WHY WE STILL CARE

☆ **Patty Hearst popularized the use of "Stockholm syndrome" as a legal defense.** Stockholm syndrome is a survival method in which a captive will begin to identify with and even defend his or her captors, which is what Hearst claimed happened to her. The syndrome was initially named after a 1973 bank robbery in Stockholm,

THE AFTERMATH

Patty Hearst: After two years in prison, President Jimmy Carter allowed Hearst to be released. She married Bernard Shaw, a San Francisco police officer, in 1979, and published a best-selling memoir called *Every Secret Thing* in 1982. Hearst also went on to play small parts in a number of movies by cult filmmaker John Waters, including *Cecil B. Demented*, which was loosely based on her abduction. In 2001, President Bill Clinton gave her a full pardon for her crime.

The SLA: The arrest of the four SLA members—Bill and Emily Harris, Wendy Yoshimura, and Steven Soliah—effectively put an end to the SLA. (Six other SLA members had died in a shootout with LAPD officers months earlier, and the rest of the members went underground.) The Harris couple got eight years in jail for kidnapping Hearst. Soliah was acquitted of all charges in the bank robbery, and Yoshimura was given immunity for the bank robbery charges in exchange for testifying against her fellow SLA members.

Sweden, during which hostages showed loyalty and affection to their captors after the captors were arrested.

☆ **The SLA gave American activists a bad name.** In the 1960s, political activism was seen as a good thing—people fighting for civil rights and protesting against American involvement in the Vietnam War. But as time wore on, radical "activist" groups like the SLA were becoming violent and losing sight of their initial missions. Hearst's kidnapping left many people with little tolerance for activists of any kind.

MORE *FAMOUS PEOPLE* DEFENDED BY F. LEE BAILEY

➡ *Sam Sheppard.* Sheppard was convicted of brutally killing his pregnant wife in 1954. By the time Bailey was hired to represent Sheppard in 1966, he had already spent 12 years in jail for his wife's murder. Bailey argued all the way up to the Supreme Court for an appeal. The guilty decision was overturned and Sheppard was awarded a new trial, which he won. Sheppard and his trials later became the basis for the TV show and movie *The Fugitive*.

➡ *Albert DeSalvo.* DeSalvo was arrested for a series of sexual assaults in Boston in 1967. Before the trial, he confessed to a psychiatrist that he was also the "Boston Strangler," who was responsible for the unsolved rape and murder of 13 women earlier in the decade. There wasn't enough evidence to try DeSalvo as the Boston Strangler, so at the sexual assault trial,

Bailey tried to use DeSalvo's confession to prove he was not guilty by reason of insanity. The tactic didn't work. The jury found DeSalvo guilty of all charges. He was killed by a prison inmate in 1973 while serving his sentence.

➡ *Ernest Medina.* Medina was the Army Captain who led US troops throughout the infamous Mai Lai massacre during the Vietnam War. His company went to the village to look for Vietcong soldiers, but it only found unarmed villagers. Still, the US troops killed over 100 of the villagers. In 1971, Bailey defended Medina at his court martial by saying that Medina didn't order the mass killings, and he was acquitted on all counts.

➡ *OJ Simpson.* Bailey was part of the "dream team" of attorneys assembled to defend football superstar OJ Simpson, who was charged with killing his ex-wife and her friend in a highly publicized 1994 trial (page 186).

DIRECTOR ROMAN POLANSKI GETS CONVICTED OF RAPE AND FLEES COUNTRY 1977

THE SCOOP!

Famous director Roman Polanski fled the US to avoid jail time after drugging and allegedly raping a girl young enough to be his daughter.

WHAT WENT DOWN

Polish-born director Roman Polanski made it big in Hollywood with a string of award-winning movies, like *Rosemary's Baby*, *Chinatown*, and a dark adaptation of *Macbeth*. He was a photographer, too, and while he was in LA in February of 1977, 43-year-old Polanski was introduced to 13-year-old aspiring actress Samantha Gailey. Polanski felt Gailey would make a good photo subject and asked her mother if he could photograph the young girl for *French Vogue*. According to Gailey's grand jury testimony two months later, Polanski asked her to pose topless during the private photo shoot. And although she felt uncomfortable, she agreed, thinking the shoot would help further her acting career. Gailey never told her mother about the topless photos, and even agreed to a second photo shoot a month later.

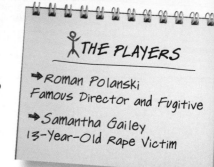

THE PLAYERS

→ Roman Polanski
Famous Director and Fugitive

→ Samantha Gailey
13-Year-Old Rape Victim

For the second shoot, Gailey said Polanski took her to actor Jack Nicholson's house (Nicholson wasn't home at the time). There, he photographed her drinking champagne and encouraged her to drink a lot of it. To help her "relax," he gave her part of a quaalude (a popular party drug in the 1960s and '70s), which she took. After taking a few topless photos, he told Gailey to pose naked in the hot tub. She did. Soon after, Polanski put his camera down, took off his clothes, jumped in the tub, and started putting the moves on her. According to Gailey's statement, she kept asking to be taken home and even faked being asthmatic, but Polanski ignored her and took her into the bedroom, where he started having sex with her. He asked if she was taking birth control pills (she wasn't), and so he switched to anal sex.

That night, Gailey told her boyfriend she had been raped. Gailey's sister overheard them and told her mom, who called the police. Less than two weeks later, Polanski was indicted on a list of charges, including rape by use of drugs, perversion, sodomy, a lewd and lascivious act upon a child under 14, and furnishing a controlled substance to a minor. He faced up to 50 years in prison. Because Polanski was a Hollywood celeb, the trial was sure to be in the papers every day. To avoid a highly publicized trial, Gailey and the prosecutors agreed

Roman Polanski at a press conference after the incident occurred.

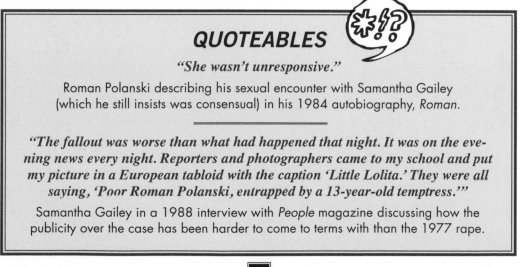

QUOTEABLES

"She wasn't unresponsive."

Roman Polanski describing his sexual encounter with Samantha Gailey (which he still insists was consensual) in his 1984 autobiography, *Roman*.

"The fallout was worse than what had happened that night. It was on the evening news every night. Reporters and photographers came to my school and put my picture in a European tabloid with the caption 'Little Lolita.' They were all saying, 'Poor Roman Polanski, entrapped by a 13-year-old temptress.'"

Samantha Gailey in a 1988 interview with *People* magazine discussing how the publicity over the case has been harder to come to terms with than the 1977 rape.

to a plea bargain: Polanski, who insisted that the sex was consensual, would plead guilty to the least serious charge—unlawful sex with a minor. But before Polanski's official sentencing in February of 1977, he fled the US and has been on the run ever since.

WHY WE STILL CARE

☆ **Roman Polanski is still a fugitive.** Other countries in Europe have provided a safe haven for Polanski, but since he fled justice after pleading guilty to unlawful sex with a minor, he's still a fugitive in the US.

THE AFTERMATH

Samantha Gailey: Despite trying to avoid a scandalous trial, Gailey's face was splashed in newspapers worldwide. The press mostly portrayed her as a teenage seductress out to ruin a powerful man's life. She gave up acting and eventually moved with her husband to Hawaii, where she became a secretary. In 1988, she sued Polanski for sexual assault and emotional distress in a civil case that was settled out of court. (He agreed to pay her $500,000 in 1993.) She's repeatedly said that the way the media has treated her over the years has been far worse than the actual rape, and she has even publicly supported Polanski returning to the US as a free man.

Roman Polanski: Polanski, who had both French and Polish citizenship, settled in Paris. France and the US have a deal that they don't have to extradite their own citizens if they don't want to (and France *doesn't* want to).

Polanski never stopped making movies. In 1980, he was nominated for an Academy Award for a movie about a sexual relationship between an older man and young girl (*Tess*). Polanski admitted to starting an affair with the lead actress, Nastassja Kinski, when she was just 15. Later, he began dating his future wife, Emmanuelle Seigner, when she was 18 and he was 51. In 2002, his movie *The Pianist* won three Oscars, including best director for Polanski, who couldn't accept the award in person because he was still not allowed into the country. In 2009, the US government worked with the Swiss government to arrest Polanski at a Zurich film festival, where he was receiving a lifetime achievement award. The Swiss government kept Polanski under house arrest for almost a year in his Swiss chalet, but set him free the summer of 2010. They refused to ship him to the States, leaving things exactly where they've been for the past 30-plus years.

☆ **Polanski fans are still trying clear his name.** In response to his 2009 arrest in Switzerland, a "Free Roman Polanski" petition was circulated denouncing the arrest, and it was signed by hundreds of Hollywood celebs, including directors Martin Scorsese, Wes Anderson, and Woody Allen (see page 57).

MORE CELEBS IN TROUBLE WITH THE LAW

➡️ *R. Kelly.* R&B star Kelly has a reputation for enjoying the company of teenage girls. (His marriage to the late singer Aaliyah had to be annulled because she was just 15 when they tied the knot.) He was already involved in four different lawsuits involving sex with underage girls in 2002 when he was arrested on 21 counts of child pornography after an anonymous source sent a video of him having sex with a young girl to the *Chicago Sun Times.* Kelly pled not guilty. Jurors had to watch the entire 27-minute sex tape, and in the end, they found Kelly not guilty of all charges.

➡️ *Charlie Sheen. Two and a Half Men* star Sheen has a long history as a Hollywood bad boy. He was first arrested in 1996 for attacking one of his girlfriends, but only got two years probation. He laid low until 2006, when his ex-wife—actress Denise Richards—slapped a restraining order on him saying he'd beat her up and threatened her life. Three years later, Sheen was arrested again for trying to choke his new wife, Brooke Mueller, but he got off with probation, rehab, and community service. Just two months out of rehab, in October of 2010, Sheen was visited by NYC police at his room at The Plaza Hotel, where they found him high, drunk, and naked, with a prostitute trapped in the bathroom. Despite the drugs, the prostitute, and the $7,000 worth of damage to the hotel room, Sheen was never charged with anything.

➡️ *Martha Stewart.* Stewart seemed to make all the right business moves, turning a catering company into a multi-million-dollar lifestyle empire with her own magazine, TV show, and line of merchandise. But in 2001, she suspiciously sold over $200,000 worth of stock in the biotech company ImClone a day before bad news about the company sent its stock plummeting. The sale led to rumors of insider trading (buying or selling stock when you have the inside scoop on a company that gives you an advantage over regular investors). In 2004, a jury found Stewart guilty of conspiracy, obstruction of justice, and lying to federal investigators. She was sentenced to five months in prison and five months under house arrest.

THE SCOOP!

In the fall of 1978, a church that was supposedly founded on racial equality and social justice came to a tragic end after a mass suicide of more than 900 followers in a South American jungle.

WHAT WENT DOWN

Jim Jones was only 25 when he founded his church, the People's Temple, in 1953. He had no formal religious training, but people really responded to his message of equality and social responsibility. It was a *little* weird when Jones moved his congregation from Indiana to California in 1965 because he had a premonition about a nuclear holocaust. But Jones continued to attract a lot of members with the church's mission to help others and create a better society.

In 1971, Jones moved the People's Temple headquarters to San Francisco, where he got involved in politics by donating lots of money to local and state politicians who supported his causes. Politicians loved Jones. All he had to do was tell his 20,000 followers to attend a rally, pass out flyers, and vote for a certain candidate—and they would. California's governor, Jerry Brown, visited the People's Temple church, and San Francisco's mayor, George Moscone, put Jones on the city's Housing Authority Commission.

Then, in 1977, *New West* magazine ran an article that got people asking *a lot* of questions about the People's Temple. The article included interviews from 10 former church members

THE PLAYERS

➡ Jim Jones
People's Temple Leader

➡ Leo Ryan
Bay Area Congressman

➡ Greg Robinson, Don Harris, and Bob Brown
Murdered Members of the Press

➡ Jones' Followers
Victims of a Forced Mass Suicide

who said that Jones pressured his followers to sell their belongings and sign over their homes to him. They described creepy all-night services where Jones pretended to cure cancer. They claimed Jones beat certain members with a paddle called "the board of education" and made churchgoers fistfight or pee on each other to atone for supposed sins. Soon after the story was published, Jones and some of his followers moved to Guyana, South America, to create a utopian farming society called Jonestown.

By 1978, around a thousand people had moved to Jonestown never to be heard from again. The relatives they left behind demanded that *someone* look into what was going on. Leo Ryan, a Congressman from the San Francisco Bay Area, flew to Jonestown on November 17 with other government officials, a group of reporters, and some concerned family members. When they first arrived, things seemed fine. The church threw a huge party for the

A photo of the mass suicide at Jonestown, 1978.

QUOTEABLES

"We didn't commit suicide. We committed an act of revolutionary suicide protesting the conditions of an inhuman world."

Jim Jones' last statements from a recording found at Jonestown, the site of the mass suicides and murders.

"We were as diverse a group of people as you'll ever encounter. We were loving, passionate people. And those people shouldn't have died."

Stephen Jones, Jim Jones' son, in an interview with *Good Morning America* in 2003. He survived the Jonestown massacre because he wasn't at the Temple at the time.

visitors, and Congressman Ryan gave a short speech saying that anyone who wanted to was welcome to fly back with them.

When the visitors left Jonestown the next day, 16 churchgoers decided to join them. So they had to wait on the air field for a second plane. While waiting, a wagon full of People's Temple members pulled up and, along with Larry Layton (one of the 16 churchgoers), fired guns at everyone planning to leave. They shot Congressman Ryan, killing him along with an NBC cameraman, an NBC reporter, a *San Francisco Chronicle* photographer, and one of the defectors. Eleven others were wounded, but they survived by playing dead until the gunmen left.

Jones called the remaining Temple members together and said that if they didn't down a deadly drink (cyanide mixed with grape juice) the US government would swoop down, torture them, and destroy everything they had built. Jones made the kids go first and instructed parents to use syringes to inject the juice into the kids' mouths if they wouldn't swallow. By the end of the day, more than 900 people were dead, including Jones, who was found dead from a shot to the head. The event went down as the largest mass suicide in modern history.

THE AFTERMATH

The People's Temple: A small number of Temple members survived the mass suicide by escaping into the jungle, hiding in the compound, or being too sick to get out of bed. There was also a Temple headquarters in Georgetown, the capital of Guyana, where around 50 more church members, including Jones' sons, lived. Jones had radioed ahead that the Georgetown members should kill themselves, too. Only one woman obeyed, killing herself and her three children. Layton was brought back to America and sentenced to life in prison. He's the only person charged with any criminal acts from that day.

The Suicide: Guyanese soldiers were the first to find the members' corpses. But because bodies decompose quickly in the jungle and Jones had confiscated everyone's IDs, it was hard to figure out who was who. The bodies were flown to Dover Air Force Base in Delaware, where they stayed until they could be identified (most weren't). Unclaimed bodies were brought back to California and buried in a mass grave at Evergreen Cemetery in Oakland. There's a memorial service there every November 18 at 11:00 am, the time and day of the massacre.

WHY WE STILL CARE

☆ **The Jonestown Massacre became one of the most highly publicized news events ever.** According to a 1978 Gallup poll, 98 percent of Americans knew or read about the tragedy. Gallup polls regularly measure what people are thinking or talking about, and more people knew about what went down in Jonestown than almost any other event in Gallup poll history.

☆ **The event inspired the saying "Don't Drink the Kool Aid."** Though it was actually a Flavor Aid brand drink mixed with cyanide that killed the members of the People's Temple, the adage "drinking the Kool Aid" has become synonymous with blindly following or accepting anyone or anything. Though the saying may seem kind of disrespectful to the hundreds who lost their lives in 1978 (and the Kool Aid company doesn't like it either), it *is* good advice.

MORE DEADLY RELIGIONS

➡️ **Branch Davidians.** In 1993, this radical religious sect was involved in a bitter battle with FBI agents that resulted in a 50-day seige (see page 174).

➡️ **Heaven's Gate.** As spiritual leader of Heaven's Gate, Marshall Applewhite was waiting for a "marker" that would let him know that aliens were coming to take his soul (and the souls of his followers) to heaven in their spaceships. Applewhite's marker—the return of the comet Hale-Bopp—came in 1997. As the comet streaked overhead, Applewhite along with other Heaven's Gate members (in matching outfits, crew cuts, and sneakers) ate pudding and applesauce mixed with a heaping helping of Phenobarbital. The drugged desserts killed them, which they believed would allow their souls to hitch a ride to heaven.

➡️ **Movement for the Restoration of the Ten Commandments.** A lot of people thought the world was going to end on New Year's Eve 2000. But few took it as seriously as the leaders of the Ugandan cult the Movement for the Restoration of the Ten Commandments. The cult urged members to sell their belongings before the world ended, leaving them empty handed as the year 2000 wore on. When angry followers later complained, leaders responded by killing them. Hundreds were burned to death in a Movement church. This led to the discovery of mass graves in Uganda bringing the death toll to almost a thousand.

THE SCOOP!

San Francisco Mayor George Moscone and the first openly gay politician, Supervisor Harvey Milk, were shot to death in broad daylight in their City Hall offices by a frustrated political rival.

WHAT WENT DOWN

In 1964, *Life* magazine declared San Francisco the "gay capital of the nation." Hundreds of openly gay men and women were flocking to San Francisco, where they felt they could live without the discrimination they experienced everywhere else. This influx of gay residents helped elect Harvey Milk to San Francisco's Board of Supervisors in 1977. Milk was the first openly gay elected official in the country's history, and his big win was a huge victory for the gay community. Unfortunately, not everyone thought Milk was a hero. After his election, he received hate mail and death threats so often that he recorded a will *just in case* he was assassinated.

But Milk wasn't despised just for being gay. He also had very liberal political views, which didn't win him any conservative friends, especially on the Board of Supervisors. One of the most conservative board members was Dan White, a Vietnam veteran, ex-cop, and former fireman. While Milk was elected by the very liberal Castro district, White was elected to the board by the conservative Excelsior district.

White and Milk disagreed a lot. San Francisco's mayor, George Moscone, was a liberal, too, and usually sided with Milk on controversial issues (like when Milk proposed a city ordinance to make it illegal to fire someone for being gay). Losing to Milk and Moscone frustrated White. Plus, White couldn't support

☆ THE PLAYERS

➡ Harvey Milk
Openly Gay Politician

➡ George Moscone
Mayor of San Francisco

➡ Dan White
Conservative Politician
and Murderer

his family on the $9,600 salary of a supervisor. After less than a year on the job, White quit in November of 1978. White's resignation freaked out his supporters, who worried about losing a conservative voice in government. They convinced White to change his mind, and five days after resigning, he asked for his old job back. White thought Moscone would welcome him back, but the Mayor saw White's resignation as a chance to replace him with another liberal, giving them the majority in City Hall, and refused.

A few days later, White headed to City Hall with a gun in his pocket. He climbed into the building through a basement window to avoid the metal detector and marched up to Moscone's office where he shot the Mayor four times. Then White reloaded his gun and walked across the hall to Milk's office. He closed the door behind him and shot Milk five times. Both men died instantly, and White was in police custody within hours. He confessed to both murders, but said he hadn't planned to kill Milk and only did it after Milk "smirked" at him. That night, 30,000 people gathered for a march from the Castro—San Francisco's largest

Harvey Milk in the Gay Freedom Day Parade, months before his assasination.

QUOTEABLES

"My name is Harvey Milk and I'm here to recruit you."
Harvey Milk's famous rallying cry, and the way he began every speech.

"If a bullet should enter my brain, let that bullet destroy every closet door."
Part of the will Harvey Milk recorded in response to death threats. In the recording, he described his desire to see gay men and women come out of the closet and live openly.

gay neighborhood—to City Hall in a peaceful candlelit vigil to mourn the deaths of Harvey Milk and George Moscone.

Since White confessed, the big question at his murder trial wasn't if he did it, but how strong his sentence would be. The case seemed like a slam dunk for premeditated murder, and maybe even the death penalty. But White's defense team said White suffered from "diminished capacity" and was driven to violence by depression and paranoid thoughts of a political conspiracy. White's defense even had a psychiatrist testify that White's depression may have been worsened by his junk food diet (i.e., Twinkies and Coke). The press loved the idea of junk food driving a man crazy and White's "Twinkie defense" made national headlines. The clever argument also worked: White was found guilty of manslaughter (meaning he didn't plan to murder Milk and Moscone—it just happened) and sentenced to only eight years in prison.

THE AFTERMATH

The Murder Trial: The light manslaughter verdict enraged the gay community, and resulted in the White Night Riot, a bloody protest that started in San Francisco's Castro neighborhood and ended at City Hall. By the end of the night, protestors had set nine police cars on fire. More than 100 people were injured (many of them cops), and millions of dollars of damage was done to the city.

Harvey Milk: More than 10,000 people paid their respects to Milk and Moscone in a ceremony at City Hall. Later, Milk's ashes were wrapped in Doonesbury and Peanuts comic strips (he loved comics) and then scattered at sea. In 2008, a movie about Harvey Milk's life and murder, *Milk*, was released starring Sean Penn. In 2009, President Obama awarded Milk the Presidential Medal of Freedom (the highest civilian honor), and the same year California Governor Arnold Schwarzenegger officially made May 22 (Milk's birthday) Harvey Milk Day.

George Moscone: Moscone was widely mourned and San Francisco's largest convention center, the Moscone Center, was named after him in December of 1978, as was one of the city's elementary schools, George Moscone Elementary.

Dan White: White was released from jail in 1984. He served only five years of his eight-year sentence. A year after his release, he was found dead in his garage of a suicide. He never expressed any remorse for the murders.

☆ **After his death, Harvey Milk became a hero for gay men and women.** By being openly gay and succeeding in politics, Milk showed others in his community that they didn't have to live a lie, or worse, commit suicide (two of the most common options at the time). While people will always wonder if gay rights could have been achieved more speedily over the years if Milk hadn't been assassinated, his bravery is still an inspiration to gay men and women who continue to fight for equal rights.

☆ **Dan White's sentence made people question "diminished capacity."** Because of all the press attention on the so-called "Twinkie defense" during White's trial, there was new scrutiny of the real defense behind it: diminished capacity. The California State Legislature banned the defense in 1981.

MORE QUESTIONABLE DEFENSES

➡ **PMS.** When surgeon Dr. Geraldine Richter was pulled over for driving erratically in 1990, she responded by cursing out the state trooper and trying to kick him in the groin. He arrested her for drunk driving, but she insisted at trial that it was PMS (not the four glasses of wine she'd had before she got behind the wheel) that made her act out. Amazingly, the judge dropped all charges.

➡ **Gay Panic.** In 1998, Aaron McKinney and Russell Henderson admitted to robbing, beating, and leaving 21-year-old student Matthew Shepard tied to a fence in freezing weather. A biker found and rescued Shepard 18 hours later, but he never regained consciousness and died in the hospital. Henderson pled guilty to murder and kidnapping, but McKinney's lawyers attempted to use the "gay panic" defense. They claimed McKinney attacked Shepard (who was openly gay) after Shepard made sexual advances that triggered childhood memories of abuse, which caused McKinney to go temporarily insane. The judge didn't buy the defense and ruled that it couldn't be used in the case. McKinney was found guilty of second-degree murder, robbery, and kidnapping and sentenced to two consecutive life sentences.

➡ **Ambien.** Before going to bed one night in 2009, 22-year-old Andrew McClay chugged whiskey along with five pills of Ambien, a prescription sleep drug. Later, he was arrested for the death of his best friend, Nicole Burns, who was found dead in a pool of blood after being bludgeoned 40 times with a hammer. McClay claimed the Ambien made him black out. His Ambien defense didn't work, and he got 48 years in jail.

THE SCOOP!

In 1980 Janet Cooke wrote a heart-breaking, award-winning article for *The Washington Post* about heroin use in the projects of Washington, DC. And she made the whole thing up.

THE PLAYERS

→ Janet Cooke
Pulitzer Prize-Winning Liar

→ The Washington Post
The Newspaper That Printed Her Stories

WHAT WENT DOWN

The Washington Post, one of the most respected newspapers in the country, hired 25-year-old Janet Cooke as a staff reporter in 1979. After just nine months on the job, she came up with an idea for an article that would make her famous. Cooke had been researching the effect of heroin on Washington, DC, residents and heard about an 8-year-old boy who was enrolled in a drug treatment program. When she told one of her editors, Milton Coleman, about the boy, he said it sounded good enough to make the front page. Cooke was psyched. Getting the front page was like winning the lottery.

The story about the young boy, "Jimmy's World," ran on the front page of *The Washington Post* in September of 1980. According to the story, Jimmy was a third-grade boy who'd been addicted to heroin since he was five. He was the product of rape and lived with his mom and her drug-dealing boyfriend. His favorite subject in school (when he went) was math because he thought it would come in handy for adding up all the money he'd make when he was 11 and old enough to start dealing drugs himself. The story was so gripping and sad that people couldn't stop talking about it.

Before the article came out, Cooke's editor promised that her the kid could remain anonymous to protect him and his family. But once the story was published, people all over the country, including First Lady Nancy Reagan, demanded to know where Jimmy lived so they could help him. Cooke claimed she couldn't reveal Jimmy's true identity because his mom's boyfriend had threatened to kill her if she did, and the newspaper stood behind Cooke. Taking matters into his own hands, Washington, DC, Mayor Marion Barry put together a task force of police officers and social workers to search for Jimmy. They scoured the city for 17 days but came up empty handed. After the failed search, Barry and others started to question if Jimmy really existed. While Cooke's editors wanted to protect her, the pressure to find Jimmy was mounting. The editors suggested Cooke secretly take them to Jimmy's house so they could help him, but Cooke claimed the family had moved to Baltimore and couldn't be contacted.

An undated photo of fake story-writer Janet Cooke.

QUOTEABLES

"'Jimmy's World' was in essence a fabrication. I never encountered or interviewed an 8-year-old heroin addict. The September 28, 1980 article in **The Washington Post** *was a serious misrepresentation, which I deeply regret. I apologize to my newspaper, my profession, the Pulitzer board and all seekers of the truth."*

Janet Cooke in her official resignation letter, which was printed in *The Washington Post* after she admitted to making up Jimmy's drug-filled story.

" … There was undoubtedly also some degree of pride—we had published the story in the first place and stood by it. We probably put too much faith in the hope that maybe things were not the way so many indicators suggested they might be."

Milton Coleman, city editor of *The Washington Post*, in the April 1981 front-page story explaining why the paper ignored early signs that Janet Cooke's story was a fraud.

Despite all the controversy surrounding "Jimmy's World," Cooke's editors, including Bob Woodward (the same guy who reported on Watergate, page 110), submitted the story to the Pulitzer Prize committee. The Pulitzer is the highest honor a writer and newspaper can get, and Cooke's story won it, in the feature writing category, in 1981. But with fame comes fact checking, and Cooke's facts weren't adding up. In her bio (which all winners had to submit), she said she graduated Magna Cum Laude from Vassar, had a graduate degree from the University of Toledo, studied at the Sorbonne in Paris, and spoke four languages. But a quick background check proved Cooke only attended Vassar for a year and had a BA (not a graduate degree) from the University of Toledo.

When Cooke's editors at *The Washington Post* confronted her about her lies, she finally owned up to them and confessed that she had fabricated Jimmy and his whole sad story. She said she had initially been tipped off about a kid but couldn't find him. Feeling pressured to come up with a front page story, she made one up. After admitting to the hoax, Cooke resigned and the newspaper returned the Pulitzer Prize the next day.

THE AFTERMATH

Janet Cooke: After resigning from *The Washington Post*, Janet Cooke held a string of retail jobs, including working behind the jewelry counter at Bloomingdale's. She attempted to write for publications like *Cosmopolitan* and *Washingtonian*, but was unsuccessful. In 1996, she agreed to an exclusive interview with journalist Mike Sager (a former boyfriend and colleague at *The Washington Post*). The interview was published in *GQ* magazine. The movie rights for it were later sold for $1.6 million, though the movie has yet to be made.

The Washington Post: The paper lost some credibility after Cooke's confession and tried to win it back by running a front-page article explaining the entire "Jimmy's World" saga. It was the second longest story in the newspaper's history with a total of almost 14,000 words.

The Pulitzer Prize: After the scandal, runner-up Teresa Carpenter from the *Village Voice* claimed the Pulitzer. Ironically, one of Carpenter's winning articles was also criticized for being less than truthful. However, since it was more of an exaggeration than an outright lie, Carpenter got to keep her prize.

WHY WE STILL CARE

☆ **The scandal revealed to the public the negative effects of competitive journalism.** Newspapers, like any business, need to make money. They do so by hiring the top reporters and trying to run the best (and juiciest) stories. This practice makes journalists highly competitive. Like many writers after her (see sidebar), Janet Cooke felt pressure to come up with a great story—even when there wasn't one.

☆ **The scandal forced newspapers and magazines to question the use of confidential sources.** If a reporter can promise to keep a source's identity a secret, they're more likely to get better, juicier information. For example, *The Washington Post* used a secret source who helped expose criminal activity during the Watergate scandal (page 110). But if a reporter has confidential sources, it makes it hard to check whether or not she has the facts straight—or is relying on any facts at all.

MORE WRITERS WITH FAKE STORIES

➡ **Stephen Glass.** Glass was a young, hotshot feature writer at *The New Republic* who always seemed to find the best magazine stories. Unfortunately, his so-called sources weren't real people. To cover up his lies, Glass wrote fake notes and created fake voicemails, websites, and business cards for his fake sources. But he was found out in 1998 when Forbes.com tried to do a follow up story on one of his articles and couldn't verify a single fact. Glass was forced to quit journalism, but in 2003 he released a book about his fakery called *The Fabulist*. A movie about him called *Shattered Glass* was released that same year.

➡ **James Frey.** Frey's drug rehab memoir, *A Million Little Pieces,* sold 3.5 million copies when Oprah made it one of her book club selections in 2005. But when thesmokinggun.com started comparing the book with Frey's real life, it looked more like fiction than fact. At first Oprah defended Frey, but as it became obvious that he had lied to her, she unleashed a televised verbal beat down that would scare anyone from making the Queen of all Media look bad ever again.

➡ **JT LeRoy.** LeRoy wrote two critically acclaimed books about prostitution and drug abuse. For ten years, fans, celebrities, and even LeRoy's agent and editor thought he was a drug-addicted, HIV-positive, teenage cross-dresser and truck stop prostitute adopted by a San Francisco couple in 1993 until his adopted mother Laura Albert was exposed as the real LeRoy. She kept up the ruse by communicating mainly by phone and having her longtime boyfriend's half-sister pose as LeRoy in public wearing a wig and sunglasses.

VANESSA WILLIAMS STEPS DOWN AS MISS AMERICA

1984

THE SCOOP!

Vanessa Williams made headlines when she was crowned the first African American Miss America, but when nude photos of her were released courtesy of porn mag *Penthouse*, pageant officials forced her to give up her crown.

WHAT WENT DOWN

African-American women weren't even allowed to compete in the Miss America pageant until 1970. So when Vanessa Williams was crowned the first black Miss America in September of 1983, it was a big deal. (First runner-up Suzette Charles was also African American.) Williams' historical win was celebrated by the African American community, but she was also the first Miss America to receive hate mail and death threats.

Despite the haters, Williams was booked for more publicity appearances during her reign than any previous winner, and earned $125,000 in appearance fees alone. But ten months after her coronation, *Penthouse* magazine dropped a bomb. In July of 1984, the magazine's publisher, Bob Guccione, announced that he had naked photos of Williams and was going to publish them in *Penthouse*'s September issue. He'd bought the pics for an undisclosed amount from photographer Tom Chiapel, a co-owner of a modeling agency Williams worked for when she was 19.

THE PLAYERS

➤ Vanessa Williams
First Black Miss America

➤ Tom Chiapel
Sleazy Photographer

➤ Bob Guccione
Penthouse Porn Publisher

Vanessa Williams wearing her crown in 1984.

The photos showed her naked and posing in sexy positions with another naked woman fueling rumors that she was a lesbian. Williams claimed the shoot was supposed to be "artistic" and that she agreed to do it because she was "curious." She also insisted that she never signed a model release, so she thought the photos could never be printed or sold. The Miss America pageant's executive committee didn't care about her excuses, they just wanted her to return her crown. In July of 1984, the pageant's

QUOTEABLES

"I've let other women down and I've let the whole black community down, and I hate that. I made a terrible error in judgment, and I know I'll have to pay for it as long as I live. But I am not a lesbian and I am not a slut, and somehow I am going to make people believe me."

Vanessa Williams in an interview with *People* magazine in September of 1984.

"The lifting of her crown not only penalizes the young woman for a past error in judgment, but by inference, will be used to reflect upon her race. A double standard is continuously played out in America against black politicians, public figures, and others who achieve eminence."

Benjamin Hooks, executive director of the National Association for the Advancement of Colored People, in a statement released after Williams was asked to step down as Miss America.

board chairman told reporters Williams' nude photos would "seriously jeopardize and irrevocably damage" the pageant. So in another first in Miss America history, Williams was forced to step down, leaving runner-up Suzette Charles to finish her reign. And the photos were, in fact, published in *Penthouse* that September.

THE AFTERMATH

Vanessa Williams: Williams bounced back quickly. She performed in off-Broadway shows and released her first R&B album, *The Right Stuff*, in 1988. It was nominated for three Grammys including Best New Artist. Since then, she's released eight more albums. Her song "Colors of the Wind," from the Disney movie *Pocahontas*, won an Academy Award, Golden Globe, and Grammy for Best Song in a Motion Picture. Williams was also nominated for three Emmys, won a Teen Choice award for her roll as Wilhelmina Slater on *Ugly Betty*, and joined the hit show *Desperate Housewives* in 2010.

Bob Guccione: *Penthouse* made a fortune off of Williams' naked photos. The September 1984 issue sold more than 6 million copies, raking in a whopping $14 million in newsstand sales. Millions more were made when Guccione published additional naked photos of Williams in the November 1984 issue. Williams initially filed a lawsuit against *Penthouse* and Tom Chiapel but dropped it in 1986 after admitting that she actually had signed a model release for the photos.

The Pageant: Miss America officials played it safe in 1985. Prior to appearing in the pageant all contestants were required to sign a new contract promising they'd never been married, lived with a man, had a child, or been guilty of "moral turpitude" (meaning anything remotely scandalous). Pageant judges also chose squeaky clean, harp-playing Mormon Sharlene Wells to be the next Miss America.

photos when the pageant publicizes contestants' body measurements as part of the event and requires them to parade in front of judges in bathing suits and high heels.

☆ **The scandal was an early lesson that scandalous pictures never go away.** When Williams decided to take some naked photos when she was 19, she probably didn't think the whole world would be seeing them later. The same is true for any teen today who allows racy pics of themselves to be taken with digital or cell-phone cameras and are surprised when those photos wind up floating around the web. The lesson: Photos are forever.

MORE PAGEANT DRAMA

➡ *Miss USA 2006 Tara Conner.* Conner got in trouble only eight months into her reign as Miss USA, reportedly partying at nightclubs, drinking, doing drugs, and even publicly making out with Miss Teen USA Katie Blair. Donald Trump (who owns the Miss Universe Pageant) met with Conner and decided the girl deserved a second chance. Conner was allowed to keep her title, but agreed to check into rehab.

➡ *Miss Universe 2008 Dayana Mendoza.* Shortly after she was crowned, semi-naked photos of Mendoza surfaced. But Miss Universe officials decided the pics were more artistic than pornographic, so she was allowed to keep her crown. However, Mendoza got in trouble again, this time with her clothes on. After visiting the American naval base in Cuba's Guantanamo Bay, which houses a controversial American prison camp, she blogged about a subsequent trip to the naval base's beaches and bars. The Miss Universe organization pulled the blog post and apologized for her insensitivity, but again decided she could keep her crown.

➡ *Miss California 2009 Carrie Prejean.* After taking a stance against same-sex marriage during the Q & A portion of the Miss USA pageant and pissing off openly gay judge Perez Hilton, Prejean (who wound up being runner-up in the contest) faced some controversy. But the real controversy started when topless photos of her surfaced on the gossip site thedirty.com, followed by eight sex tapes Prejean had sent to a boyfriend years before. In the end, Prejean was asked to step down as Miss California, but it was actually for refusing to show up at Miss California events, not for being naked or opposing gay marriage.

➡ *Miss England 2009 Rachel Christie.* Christie, who was the first black Miss England, was dethroned after getting arrested for hitting Miss Manchester, Sara Jones, at a porn-themed party at a night club in Manchester, England. The two beauty queens were fighting over a muscle-bound guy from the TV show *Gladiators*.

THE SCOOP!

Bernhard Goetz, a 37-year-old white man, shot four unarmed African American teenagers on a New York City subway car. Some New Yorkers saw him as a hero who took a stand against the city's lawlessness; others thought he was a cold-blooded killer who got away with murder.

WHAT WENT DOWN

It was 1984, and New York City was in the middle of a serious crime wave. Muggings, robberies, and homicides had become a frighteningly common occurrence, especially on the city's subways. Three days before Christmas, native New Yorker Bernhard "Bernie" Goetz, 37, was sitting in a subway car when an African American teen approached Goetz and asked him for five dollars. The teen, Troy Canty, was with three friends: Barry Allen, Darrell Cabey, and James Ramseur.

Goetz had been mugged and beaten before—and by black youths—and didn't wait for it to happen again. He pulled out an unlicensed gun he'd carried since his last mugging and shot the four teens. They were all severely wounded (but none died), and it was total chaos in the car. Goetz refused to hand over his gun to the train driver (who had stopped the train). Instead, he jumped out on to the tracks, and ran through the subway tunnel and up on to the streets. He hid in New England until December 30, when he finally turned himself in to the New Hampshire police.

THE PLAYERS

➡ Bernhard Goetz
Subway Vigilante

➡ Troy Canty, Barry Allen, Darrell Cabey, and James Ramseur
The Teens He Shot

Bernhard Goetz in 2008 at a Vegetarian Pride Parade.

During the two-hour police interrogation, Goetz recounted his mugging three years earlier and claimed that New York City was "lawless," and that all citizens should be armed because the police and justice system were not doing anything to keep people safe. He said he was forced to take matters into his own hands. When Goetz's confession hit newspapers, many New Yorkers agreed with him, dubbing Goetz the Subway Vigilante. His supporters offered him money for lawyers and championed his actions in the media and at dinner parties around the country.

Goetz's critics, however, argued that he was a cold-blooded, racist criminal. In the trial that followed, Goetz faced a slew of charges—attempted murder, assault, reckless endangerment, and illegal weapons possession. But Goetz's attorneys stuck to his self-defense story. The mostly white jury bought the defense, and acquitted Goetz on everything except the unlicensed gun charge. He served just eight months in jail.

WHY WE STILL CARE

☆ **The trial is a great example of jury nullification.** Jury nullification is when a jury acquits a defendant—who is, based on the law, guilty—for reasons that don't have to do with that particular trial. In this case, Goetz was likely let off easy not because he was innocent (it really wasn't self-defense because the teens hadn't

THE AFTERMATH

The Teen Victims: Though Goetz's victims were unarmed when he shot them, they all had criminal records and all (except for Cabey, who was paralyzed for life from the gunshot wound) ended up in jail. Ramseur was involved in an especially violent gang rape, robbery, and assault of a pregnant teenager soon after the shooting. Cabey filed a civil case against Goetz that went to trial in 1996. Goetz's statements that the world would be better off if Cabey had died that day didn't go over too well with the mostly Hispanic and black jury. They awarded Cabey $43 million dollars, which Goetz (who declared bankruptcy right after the trial) hasn't paid a dime of.

Bernhard Goetz: Goetz found new causes to take up: vegetarianism and squirrels. He ran for mayor of New York City in 2001 on a platform that advocated providing vegetarian options in the city's schools, hospitals, and prisons. He received only 1,300 votes. Goetz currently builds homes in the city's parks for squirrels and cares for injured squirrels in his apartment.

New York: Crime in New York City reached its peak in 1990, but declined every year after for 15 straight years. Many attributed the decline to the New York Police Department, which had put more officers on the streets and established new procedures to combat rampant violence. By 2005, The Big Apple was the safest big city in the country; 2009 saw the lowest number of murders since 1963.

attacked him and weren't armed) but because the jurors were all so fed up with crime (especially on the subways) they were willing to look the other way. The murder trial of Sacco and Vanzetti (page 46) is another example of jury nullification.

☆ **The scandal put a spotlight on crime in NYC.** In the 1980s, the streets and subways of New York City were so dangerous that people (black and white) were cheering on a man for shooting four teenagers in front of a crowd of witnesses. Many see the Goetz case as a tipping point that prompted government and law enforcement officials to take crime prevention more seriously. Over the years, their efforts have turned New York City into one of the safest big cities in the world.

MORE AMERICAN VIGILANTES

➡ *Montana Vigilantes.* In the early 1860s, the gold-mining towns of Montana were overrun by a group of outlaws, ironically called the Innocents. At the end of 1863, in the gold-mining town of Virginia City, a group of citizens got together to put a stop to them. In just two months, they rounded up and hung 24 Innocents who they decided were guilty, cleaning up most of the crime in the area.

➡ *Jack Ruby.* On November 22, 1963, President John F. Kennedy was publically shot and killed in Dallas, Texas, shocking the nation. Lee Harvey Oswald was arrested shortly after for the murder. When Oswald was being moved to more secure jail cell two days later, night-club owner Ruby pushed to the front of the gathered crowd and shot Oswald dead. Ruby was found guilty of murder and sentenced to death, though many Americans saw him as a hero avenging the death of their beloved president. Ruby died of cancer while waiting for his second trial.

➡ *Chris Simcox.* In 2001, anti–illegal immigration civilian Simcox decided that the federal government wasn't doing enough to keep illegal immigrants from crossing the Arizona–Mexico border. So he spearheaded the Civil Homeland Defense Corps, a volunteer (mostly armed) patrol group, to help monitor the border for illegal crossings. Though some Americans saw the group as patriots protecting the country, many— including President George W. Bush and Mexican President Vincente Fox—accused it of vigilantism, but because their actions never broke any laws, they were never arrested.

THE SCOOP!

After more than 20 years of praising the Lord on TV, televangelist Jim Bakker was brought down by two cardinal sins—swindling millions of dollars from loyal followers and having sex in a Florida hotel room with a church secretary.

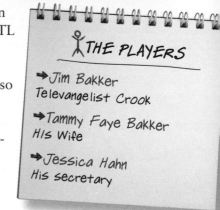

THE PLAYERS

→ Jim Bakker
Televangelist Crook

→ Tammy Faye Bakker
His Wife

→ Jessica Hahn
His secretary

WHAT WENT DOWN

Televangelist Jim Bakker gained a loyal following over almost 30 years preaching the "prosperity gospel," which taught that material things are a blessing from God. To get on God's good side, he said, all you had to do was pray—and pledge money to one of God's spiritual representatives, like Bakker. He and his wife, Tammy Faye, hosted the popular TV show *The PTL Club* (PTL stood for "Praise the Lord" or "People That Love"). The show started in 1976 and was a Sunday sermon, talk show, and fundraiser rolled into one. It ran on The PTL network (which Bakker also owned), and was made possible by financial support from viewers, who were tearfully urged on air by Jim and Tammy Faye to contribute to the ministry's good works.

Jim and Tammy Faye lived a lavish lifestyle. They owned six houses, a 55-foot houseboat, a fleet of fancy cars, and an air-conditioned dog house. This lifestyle encouraged critics who said that PTL really stood for "Pass the Loot"—but the Bakkers maintained a loyal, paying following. One of Bakker's fundraisers on *The PTL Club* was selling $1,000 a pop "lifetime membersips." The partnerships (which he claimed were God's idea) bought

Photo of Jim Bakker taken during the scandal, 1987.

you three nights per year for life at the new luxury hotels Bakker was building at Heritage USA, his Christian theme park.

But in 1987 Bakker fell on some bad luck. Threatened with blackmail by "his enemies," he was forced to admit that he'd had a sexual encounter in a Florida hotel room with a 21-year-old church secretary named Jessica Hahn. Bakker said that Hahn used "womanly tricks" to seduce him. Hahn, on the other hand, said she'd been brought to Florida to watch Bakker's kids, but was then drugged and raped by Bakker and an associate. (She said she never filed charges out of respect for PTL's mission.)

A disgraced Bakker handed over control of the PTL ministry to rival Baptist televangelist Jerry Falwell. When Falwell took a good look at the PTL accounting

QUOTEABLES

"Excess and success are close together. Anyone who is successful has got to be excessive."

Jim Bakker in a 1985 interview with the *New York Times*.

"[Bakker has made the PTL] probably the greatest scab and cancer on the face of Christianity in 2,000 years of Church history."

Jerry Falwell speaking out against Jim Bakker in a televised news conference in October of 1987 after the PTL had declared bankruptcy.

books, he found more problems: In 1987, the PTL had taken in $4.2 million a month, but spent $7.2 million. And the "lifetime partnerships" were fraudulent. Bakker sold tens of thousands of them, but had only built one 500-room hotel. The PTL was on the brink of going bankrupt, and $265,000 in ministry funds had gone to (try to) keep Hahn quiet. Bakker was defrocked by the Assemblies of God and convicted on 24 counts of fraud and conspiracy for cheating 116,000 of his followers out of an astounding $158 million. He was fined $500,000 and sentenced to 45 years in jail.

THE AFTERMATH

Jim Bakker: His sentence was eventually lowered to 18 years, and he was paroled after just five. In 1997, Bakker published his memoir, *I Was Wrong*, detailing the rise and fall of the PTL and his time in jail. He renounced the prosperity gospel, and in 1998 published *Prosperity and the Coming Apocalypse*, which warned readers about materialism and the end of times.

Tammy Faye Bakker: Tammy Faye ended her 30-year marriage to Jim while he was in jail. She later married Rob Messner, the lead contractor for Heritage USA.

Jessica Hahn: Hahn sold her story and semi-naked shots of herself to *Playboy* magazine for $1 million, which she may have needed since a judge forced her to return her PTL hush money. Hahn later offered to help PTL with fundraising, but the ministry declined.

The PTL: Throughout the scandal, many members of Bakker's flock stood behind him. Dozens of those defrauded by his "lifetime partnerships" scam even testified in Bakker's defense at his trial. But without Bakker as the head of the PTL, donations dropped dramatically. The organization was forced to declare bankruptcy in 1989 with a debt of $130 million. Then, the IRS revoked the PTL's tax-exempt status (the organization had been exempt from paying taxes because it was supposed to be a nonprofit religious organization, which it obviously wasn't) and demanded $55 million in back taxes. The amount was way more than the PTL could afford. The PTL television studios, network, and Heritage USA theme park were sold at auction to a Canadian real estate developer, leaving nothing of the empire the Bakkers built.

WHY WE STILL CARE

⭐ **The prosperity gospel that Bakker popularized still lives on today.** Though the PTL scandal momentarily tarnished the shine of prosperity gospel in the '80s, the philosophy has been revived under new names like "health and wealth," "name it and claim it," and "prosperity lite." The basic principle is: God wants you to make good money.

⭐ **The scandal affected people's trust in televangelists.** In the fallout from the Bakker scandal, the bank accounts and viewership for all televangelists were hit hard as their flocks grew distrustful of their accounting. Donations and viewership have since rebounded, but the ministries never regained the popularity they had in the 1980s. Some are more wary of giving money to ministries in general, because there's still no way to tell where the money is going since religious entities are exempt from being taxed and regulated by the government.

MORE SERIOUS SINNERS

➡ **Billy James Hargis.** This ultra-conservative televangelist founded the equally conservative American Christian College in 1971 and even went on tour with its choir, the All-American Kids. Hargis seemed like a saint until members of the choir, male and female, came forward with tales of coerced sex. Hargis claimed that his enemies—Satan and the Communists—had teamed up to bring him down.

➡ **Jimmy Swaggart.** In 1986, popular and competitive televangelist Swaggart outed fellow televangelist Martin Gorman for having an affair getting him defrocked. But Gorman got back at Swaggart with a $90 million defamation suit and pictures of Swaggart bringing a prostitute back to a New Orleans motel room. When Swaggart's sex scandal was revealed, he was defrocked, too. Swaggart was caught by police again with another prostitute three years later.

➡ **Ted Haggard.** President of the National Association of Evangelicals (NAE) and founder of a mega-church in Colorado Springs, Haggard was a religious celebrity with famous friends like President George W. Bush. Then, in 2006, a male prostitute saw Haggard on TV promoting a ban on gay marriage in Colorado, and recognized Haggard as a man who had been paying him for sex. The prostitute went public with the info and claimed Haggard also liked meth. Haggard was forced to resign from the NAE and was fired by his church.

THE SCOOP!

Pete Rose is arguably one of the greatest baseball players of all time, but gambling (and lying about it) in 1989 got him banned from Major League Baseball—for life.

WHAT WENT DOWN

From the 1960s to 1980s, Pete Rose racked up a long list of baseball accomplishments: He won three World Series rings, was voted an All-Star 17 times (playing five different positions), and still holds the Major League Baseball record for the most hits, games played, and at bats. In 1984, he became manager of the Cincinnati Reds (the team he played with for most of his career) while still on the team. He remained the Reds' manager after retiring as a player two years later in 1986.

THE PLAYERS

➡ Pete Rose
Baseball Player and Gambler

➡ John Dowd
Hired Attorney

➡ Bartlett Giamatti
Major League Baseball Commissioner

While he was managing the Reds, rumors started to circulate that Rose not only had a nasty gambling problem but was betting on baseball (one of the worst league rules you can break). In May of 1989, Baseball Commissioner Bartlett Giamatti hired an attorney, John Dowd, to look into the rumors. Dowd's report was supposed to remain secret, but it was leaked to the media and full of evidence that Rose was betting tens of thousands of dollars (per day!) on horse racing, pro football, college basketball, and, yes, even baseball. Worst of all, there was evidence that Rose was betting on his own team, the Reds (though always to win).

Pete Rose in his Cincinnati Reds uniform in the 1970s.

Despite all the proof, Rose repeatedly denied ever gambling on baseball, even while Commissioner Giamatti moved forward with hearings to prove Rose was guilty. Rose responded by filing a lawsuit against Giamatti to block the hearings. Then in August of 1989, after a summer of legal wrangling, Rose and Giamatti signed a deal stipulating that Giamatti would call off the hearings and Rose would be banned from baseball (including stepping down as manager of the Reds) and put on the "ineligible list." The deal prevented any official ruling on Rose's guilt, which is what he was

QUOTEABLES

"I'd be willing to bet you, if I were a betting man, that I have never bet on baseball."

Pete Rose in an interview with *Sports Illustrated* during the beginning of the investigation into rumors of his gambling.

"I bet on baseball in 1987 and 1988 ... It's time to clean the slate. It's time to take responsibility. I'm 14 years late."

Pete Rose in the January 2004 interview with Charles Gibson, where he first publicly admitted to betting on baseball.

trying to avoid, even though everyone knew he was guilty. The agreement also included a clause that would allow Rose to apply to be reinstated after a year, but any reinstatement would be under the discretion of the baseball commissioner.

Soon after the ban was put in effect, Rose was separately convicted on federal charges of tax evasion, sentenced to five months in federal prison, fined $50,000, and required to complete 1,000 hours of community service. Things definitely weren't looking good for Rose, but he was still banking on making it into the National Baseball Hall of Fame, which players become eligible for five years after they retire. Rose would have been eligible in 1992. But, in 1991 the Hall of Fame passed a new rule saying no player on the "ineligible list" could be inducted, meaning Rose, despite being one of the greatest players in history, wouldn't get in unless the ban was lifted.

THE AFTERMATH

Pete Rose: Rose and his supporters tirelessly campaigned to get the baseball ban lifted, but Rose refused to admit he had bet on baseball for years after the scandal. In 2002, however, he finally admitted to then Baseball Commissioner Bud Selig that he bet on the game. He was hoping his confession would get the ban lifted, but it didn't work. In 2004, Rose made a more public confession on *Good Morning America* while promoting his new book, *Pete Rose: My Prison Without Bars*. The confession coincided with the announcement of that year's Baseball Hall of Fame inductees (a list that obviously didn't include Rose). Many saw the timing as a publicity ploy, and thought Rose apologized as a stunt. It didn't bring him any closer to getting back into baseball. He now makes a living signing baseballs and selling memorabilia. The bat he used to break the all-time hit record sold for $158,776 (much less than expected).

WHY WE STILL CARE

☆ **Sports writers say the scandal changed the Baseball Hall of Fame's rules.** Though the board members of the Baseball Hall of Fame insisted that their 1991 decision to keep players on the ineligible list out of the Hall of Fame had nothing to do with Pete Rose, most sports writers (and fans) don't believe them. They passed the rule, which is still in effect, the year before Rose would have been eligible for induction, and, at the time, he was the only living player on the ineligible list.

☆ **Many people today think baseball was too hard on Pete Rose—and too easy on current rule-breakers.** While it's true that Rose frequently bet on baseball, it's unlikely that his actions ever changed the outcome of a game. He wasn't throwing games like the eight Chicago White Sox players in 1919 (page 26), he was simply betting on them. Meanwhile, more recent baseball superstars like Mark McGwire and Barry Bonds have used performance-enhancing drugs, which totally influence the outcome of games, and these players have faced very few consequences.

MORE SCANDALS THAT ROCKED PRO BASEBALL

➡ ***Black Sox.*** In 1919, eight members of the White Sox (nicknamed the Black Sox) made a deal with gamblers to throw the World Series, resulting in one of the biggest scandals in sports history (page 26).

➡ ***Baseball Strike.*** In the middle of the 1994 baseball season, players went on strike to protest proposed salary caps, even though the average player was making $1.8 million at the time. The strike lasted 234 days, canceling the 1994 World Series and the beginning of the 1995 season. Fans were annoyed that players and owners ruined the season because they couldn't agree about money, and it took a long time for fans to return to the games in pre-strike numbers.

➡ ***BALCO Labs.*** In 2003, federal agents raided a San Francisco Bay Area lab called BALCO, which had been manufacturing and distributing undetectable steroids to some of the world's greatest athletes. Both Mark McGwire and Barry Bonds, who had each broken the single-season home run record (in 1998 and 2001, respectively), were accused of using performance enhancing drugs from this lab, and the raid prompted the House of Representatives to hold hearings into the use of steroids in the sport.

THE SCOOP!

When famous artist Robert Mapplethorpe died, a new exhibit of his work—which contained several graphic photos of naked men—started a battle between museums, artists, and the government.

WHAT WENT DOWN

Photographer Robert Mapplethorpe is famous for his early black-and-white Polaroids, beautiful still-life shots of flowers, and portraits of famous friends like rock 'n' roller Patti Smith, pop star Debbie Harry, and artist Andy Warhol. Mapplethorpe, who was openly gay, also took photos of naked and leather-clad men in unusual sexual positions, but these works were lesser known until 1989.

That year, Mapplethorpe died of AIDS-related illnesses, and the Institute of Contemporary Art in Philadelphia (ICA) put together a retrospective exhibit of his work. It included some of Mapplethorpe's pictures that had both homosexual and sexually bizarre themes (like a photo of a man peeing into another man's mouth and a naked self-portrait of Mapplethorpe with a bull whip coming out of his butt). The exhibit's first two stops, in Philadelphia and Chicago, didn't cause much of a stir. But by the time the exhibit reached the Corcoran Gallery of Art in Washington, DC, a movement to shut it down started by conservative Christian groups who opposed the content of the sexual photos, was gaining ground.

The exhibit was partially funded by the National Endowment of the Arts (NEA), an organization that gets all of its money from

THE PLAYERS

→ Robert Mapplethorpe
Controversial (Dead)
Photographer

→ Jesse Helms
Anti-Obscenity Crusader

Robert Mapplethorpe in New York City, 1985.

the US government. Many Christian groups claimed that by allowing homosexual images into the Mapplethorpe exhibit, the government was funding and distributing porn (and even worse, homosexual porn, which the groups found especially offensive). They teamed up with conservative Republican Senator Jesse Helms who passed some of the more explicit photos around Congress to create opposition against the exhibit, the Corcoran Gallery, and the NEA. Appalled by the photos, 100 members of Congress signed a petition criticizing

QUOTEABLES

"This Mapplethorpe fellow was an acknowledged homosexual. He's dead now, but the homosexual theme goes throughout his work … If someone wants to write ugly nasty things on the men's room wall, the taxpayers do not provide the crayon."

Senator Jesse Helms in a July 28, 1989, article in the *New York Times* explaining why he thought taxpayer money shouldn't be used for Mapplethorpe's work.

"By withdrawing from the Mapplethorpe exhibition, we, the board of trustees and the director, have inadvertently offended many members of the arts community, which we deeply regret. Our course in the future will be to support art, artists, and freedom of artistic expression."

An official apology released by the Corcoran Gallery of Art in September of 1989 for canceling the Mapplethorpe exhibit.

the NEA for funding the exhibit. And even though the Mapplethorpe exhibit only got a teeny part of the NEA's annual budget ($30,000 out of a budget of almost $170 million), Congress threatened to slash the NEA's funding if it couldn't get more say in what kind of art the organization supported.

Caught in the middle of the scandal was the Corcoran, which also got a lot of its funding from the government. Afraid of losing government support and getting caught up in a political firestorm, the Corcoran cancelled the Mapplethorpe show, angering artists and free-speech activists nationwide. Artists accused the Christian groups and the Republican Senator of putting pressure on the Corcoran and trying to censor their creative freedom, which they said they had a right to under the First Amendment of the Constitution.

THE AFTERMATH

The Corcoran Gallery: The museum suffered major backlash from cancelling Mapplethorpe's exhibit. Artists boycotted it and six staff members quit in protest. Pop artist Lowell Blair Nesbitt, a close friend of Mapplethorpe's who had planned to donate more than a million dollars to the museum, changed his will and left it nothing. Six months after the show was cancelled, the Corcoran's rep was still in ruins, and director Christina Orr-Cahall resigned hoping it would help rehab the museum's image. But the Corcoran will always be linked with this scandal.

The Mapplethorpe Exhibit: After the Corcoran scandal, Mapplethorpe's photos caused more problems at Cincinnati's Contemporary Art Center. Just hours after the controversial exhibit opened there, police arrested Dennis Barrie, the Art Center's art director, and seized seven Mapplethorpe photographs they found especially offensive. Barrie and the museum were put on trial on obscenity charges. It was the first time any museum had to go to court for art it displayed, but both were found not guilty. Meanwhile, the controversy over the photos drove huge crowds to see the exhibit. In Cincinnati, 81,000 people bought tickets to the show. In comparison, only 40,000 people total visited the museum during all of 2009. Sales of Mapplethorpe's work almost doubled, cementing his place in the art world as one of the country's most influential photographers.

WHY WE STILL CARE

☆ **The scandal created an ongoing debate about how much control the government should have over the art it funds.** In response to the scandal, Congress passed a provision that stipulated that the government (meaning the NEA) could only fund art that met "general standards of decency." Many controversial artists were denied grants as a result, and they fought back. In 1996, a federal appeals court overturned the provision, citing it as a violation of the right to free speech. Two years later, the Supreme Court ruled that the decency standard was Constitutional and reinstated the provision. Artists are still fighting to repeal it today.

☆ **Mapplethorpe's photos brought gay-themed art into the limelight.** Though there were already openly gay artists in the 1980s, gay-themed art (depicting gay men and lesbians) was still considered generally unacceptable. Mapplethorpe's photographs set the stage for other artists to publically explore gay themes in their work.

MORE ART UNDER FIRE

➡ **Piss Christ *by Andres Serrano.*** Released in 1987, this photograph of a plastic crucifix suspended in a glass of the artist's pee caused a scandal around the same time as Mapplethorpe's retrospective. The works of the two photographers are frequently linked because Serrano also received NEA funding and scorn from Republican Senator Jesse Helms.

➡ ***"Immediate Family" by Sally Mann.*** In 1992, photographer Sally Mann released a collection of mostly nude photos of her three young children called "Immediate Family." While the art world saw the collection as a mother's touching account of the innocence of childhood, others just saw child porn. Before publishing a book of the series, Mann showed the photos to the FBI to make sure she wouldn't be prosecuted. The FBI gave her the go ahead and the photos made her famous.

➡ **The Holy Virgin Mary *by Chris Ofili.*** New York City mayor Rudy Giuliani had a problem with pretty much all of the art included in the Brooklyn Museum's "Sensation" exhibit in 1999. But he had a special dislike for British Nigerian Ofili's depiction of the Virgin Mary: a black woman with an exposed breast covered in elephant poop, with small pictures of female genitalia and butts in the background. Giuliani publicly questioned the museum's fundraising techniques, and tried to get it evicted and cut off its funding for six months. He finally coughed up the funds after the courts ruled in favor of the museum.

THE SCOOP!

The pop group Milli Vanilli, headed by Rob Pilatus and Fab Morvan, won the Grammy for best new artist of 1989. But just eight months later, Pilatus and Morvan became the joke of the music industry, were forced to return their Grammy, and were indicted in at least 22 different lawsuits.

WHAT WENT DOWN

The pop band Milli Vanilli took the US by storm in 1989. Their first album, Girl You Know It's True, with its catchy mix of dance, electro-pop, and rap, quickly became a crazy success in the US. Not only did the album go platinum six times, it also had three number one Billboard hits—"Blame it on the Rain," "Girl I'm Gonna Miss You," and "Baby Don't Forget My Number." As a result of the album's popularity, the group's two vocalists, the dreadlocked and be-spandexed hotties

Rob Pilatus and Fab Morvan, became superstars, winning a Grammy and three American Music Awards in one year.

THE PLAYERS

➡ Franz Farian
German Music Producer

➡ Rob Pilatus
Lip Syncing Pop Star #1

➡ Fab Morvan
Lip Syncing Pop Star #2

Then, during an MTV performance at a theme park in Connecticut during the summer of 1989, something strange happened. There was a glitch with the sound system, and during the song "Girl You Know It's True," the line "girl you know it's …" repeated over and over again through the speakers. Pilatus and Morvan initially tried to sing and dance along, but it soon became clear that the music wasn't coming from them—it was coming from a prerecorded track; the duo ran off stage. Suddenly, everyone—especially music journalists—were asking questions about whether or not Pilatus and Morvan actually were the voices of Milli Vanilli.

Franz Farian, Milli Vanilli's producer, along with Pilatus and Morvan, denied accusations that the band might be lip-syncing for more than a year. But in November of 1990, Farian—under pressure from the press and from Pilatus and Morvan (who were pushing to sing on the next release)—finally issued a statement admitting that Pilatus and Morvan weren't the vocal artists for Milli Vanilli.

It turns out that Farian had created the dance-pop act that became Milli Vanilli in the late 1980s, hoping it would be a big hit in the European Club scene. The act was made up of a collection of musicians, including multiple vocalists. The band made its first album, All or Nothing, in Europe in 1988. Farian decided to put Pilatus and Morvan, two dancer/models from the Munich club scene, on the album's cover and have

Fab Morvan and Rob Pilatus performing as Milli Vanilli in Italy, 1989.

QUOTEABLES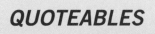

"Musically, we are more talented than any Bob Dylan ... we are more talented than Paul McCartney. Mick Jagger ... I'm the new modern rock 'n' roll. I'm the new Elvis."

Rob Pilatus in a March 1990 interview with *Time* magazine, eight months before Farian came clean about the lip syncing

---

"We were living together in the projects, with two other musicians in Munich. We had nothing to eat, and we were unhappy. We wanted to be stars. And suddenly this guy gave us a chance, and we took it."

Rob Pilatus in November of 1990 at a press conference (just after the band's Grammy was revoked) explaining why he agreed to be part of the hoax.

them perform at appearances to prerecorded music. He thought their good looks and club style would make the album more popular and marketable than the real performers. (Pilatus and Morvan were also aspiring musicians but didn't perform anything on the album.) Sure enough, Milli Vanilli became a huge hit in Europe.

Soon, the American record company Arista, noticing Milli Vanilli's success, signed the duo, remixed the album, and released it under the name Girl You Know It's True. As far as American fans had been concerned, Pilatus and Morvan were Milli Vanilli. Later, Arista claimed it never knew that Pilatus and Morvan weren't the real singers, though Pilatus and Morvan claimed Arista did.

Milli Vanilli was hardly the first band to be fronted by performers who were seen as more marketable than the actual musicians, but because they won a Grammy, sold so many records, and become so popular, the fake-out wasn't taken lightly by the public or the press. By the end of 1990, Milli Vanilli was forced to return its Grammy by the National Academy of Recording Arts and Sciences (the people who give out Grammys). Despite attempts at a comeback, Pilatus and Morvan faded into obscurity, remaining a symbol of how superficial the music world is.

THE AFTERMATH

The Band: After the scandal broke in 1990, Pilatus and Morvan created a band called *Rob & Fab* and released a self-titled album, *Rob & Fab,* on which they actually sang. It was not a success. The second Milli Vanilli album was ready for release at the time the scandal broke, and Farian released it as *The Real Milli Vanilli*. It was also not very successful.

Rob Pilatus: Pilatus, unfortunately, struggled with substance abuse, and wound up spending time in jail for assault and vandalism. In 1998, he was found dead at 33 in a Frankfurt, Germany, hotel room from an accidental drug and alcohol overdose.

Fab Morvan: In the aftermath of the lip-syncing scandal, Morvan, ironically, became a session musician (an unaccredited musical performer for hire, much like the real vocalists behind Milli Vanilli). He also worked as a DJ and released a solo album, Love Revolution, which critics liked, though it barely sold.

WHY WE STILL CARE

★ **The scandal illustrated how focused the public is on image.** After the launch of MTV and music videos in 1981, musicians no longer had the luxury of letting their music speak for itself. A successful group had to combine music, performance, and looks to become stars.

★ **The scandal helped modern-day unaccredited artists get credited.** After the scandal, artists who sang unaccredited on albums began to demand the recognition and royalties they had coming. Martha Wash sang unaccredited lead vocals for a number of groups, including the house group Black Box's two top-ten hits, "Everybody, Everybody" and "Strike It Up," and C+C Music Factory's number one hit "Gonna Make You Sweat (Everybody Dance Now)." In the pre Milli Vanilli era, she was told she was unmarketable because of her weight, but after the scandal she successfully sued to receive credit and royalties on the songs she sang.

MORE FAMOUS PREFAB BANDS

➡ **The Funk Brothers.** For most of the songs they released, Motown Records used a group of more than 20 unaccredited studio musicians, the core of which were known as the Funk Brothers. The Funk Brothers were so prolific that, according to the 2002 documentary *Standing in the Shadows of Motown*, they performed on more number one hits than Elvis Presley, The Beatles, The Rolling Stones, and The Beach Boys combined.

➡ **The Monkees.** In 1966, the band The Monkees was created for a TV show of the same name, which was developed to capitalize on the success of the Beatles' movie *A Hard Day's Night*. The actors hired to play The Monkees on TV sang on their first two albums, but they weren't allowed to play their instruments or write the songs. When their music and TV show became popular, they pressured their management for more control, and by the third album the fictional band became a real one, playing the instruments they were cast to play on the TV show and writing their own songs. They even continued releasing new material and touring after the TV show was canceled.

THE SCOOP!

In the summer of 1990, Madonna brought music and controversy on the road in the biggest, baddest, most theatrical concert tour the world—and the Catholic Church—had ever seen.

WHAT WENT DOWN

By 1990, American pop star Madonna had built a successful music career around controversy and fearless sexuality. She wore rosaries as necklaces, showed off her cleavage, danced sexily in front of burning crosses, and made midriff tops and bare belly-buttons a style *do*. In keeping with her image, Madonna wanted her Blond Ambition World Tour to be the tour everybody talked about. And it was.

Blond Ambition was the must-see concert of the summer. It was the most high-tech show to date with five sets that went up and down on hydraulics. Madonna also worked with a choreographer to make each song its own elaborately staged theatrical performance and picked themes that were sure to hit a nerve: sex and religion. Fashion guru Jean Paul Gautier designed all of her costumes, including the concert's signature cone-shaped bras. And in case all of that didn't generate enough hype, Madonna allowed filmmakers to capture every minute of the tour for a documentary, giving viewers an all-access pass to behind-the-scenes highlights like Madonna practicing oral sex on a soda bottle.

Naturally, the tour had a lot of critics. Before Madonna's third show at the Skydome in Toronto, Canada, two detectives and a government attorney showed up backstage

✶ THE PLAYERS

➡ Madonna
Talented Troublemaker

➡ The Church
Religious Censors

after Canadian parents complained that the show was too lewd. Parents were particularly bothered by the star's performance of her hit "Like a Virgin," which she sang while rolling around on a red velvet bed in fishnets as two male dancers felt her up. At the end of the song, Madonna pretended to masturbate and enthusiastically humped the bed's pillows while lights flashed on and off. The police watched every minute to see if Madonna was violating a Canadian law that banned "immoral, indecent, or obscene performances." In the end, they decided she wasn't quite lewd enough to break any laws and left without making any arrests.

Madonna on the Blonde Ambition tour, in a conical bra.

QUOTEABLES

"My show is not a conventional rock show but a theatrical presentation of my music. And like theater, it asks questions, provokes thoughts, and takes you on an emotional journey portraying good and bad, light and dark, joy and sorrow, redemption and salvation ..."

Madonna at a 1990 press conference in Italy during which she defended her show hoping to end the boycott.

―――――――

"This is a person who has very limited assets to sell and is willing to exploit an entire community to sell more tickets."

Ian Scott, Ontario's attorney general in 1990, critiquing the Blond Ambition World Tour in the *Toronto Sun*.

Canada wasn't the only country that had issues with the concert. Madonna's love of mixing religion and sex had been angering conservative Roman Catholics for years. So by the time Blond Ambition got to Italy, Catholic groups there had joined forces with the Pope to boycott her three performances. Usually controversy worked in Madonna's favor and boosted ticket sales, but the influence of the Catholic Church in Italy was too strong. The first show in Italy was the first of the whole tour to not sell out. Madonna tried to make peace with her Italian audience. She performed wearing the jersey of a famous Italian soccer player and held a press conference defending herself and her show. Still, even scalpers had a hard time unloading tickets, and one of the Italian shows had to be canceled. The tour sold out everywhere else, though, and it's still regarded as one of the most memorable performances in music history.

THE AFTERMATH

The Tour: More than 800,000 Madonna fans flocked to see the Blond Ambition World Tour, resulting in $19.4 million dollars in gross sales. HBO also paid the pop diva $1 million to broadcast the last show of the tour live and 4.3 million households tuned in, making the concert the most watched non-sports event in HBO history at the time. In 2001, one of the Gaultier cone bras worn by the star during the controversial tour sold for $21,105 at an auction. It was the top-selling bra of all time, until a few months later, when a bra from Madonna's 1993 tour, The Girlie Show, outsold it.

Madonna: The Guinness Book of World Records lists Madonna as the Most Successful Female Recording Artist of All Time. She's won seven Grammys to date, including one for the live broadcast of Blond Ambition.

The Documentary: *Madonna: Truth or Dare,* the documentary filmed during the Blond Ambition World Tour, premiered at the Cannes Film Festival a year after the tour started and grossed $15 million. It held the record of the highest-grossing documentary for 11 years.

WHY WE STILL CARE

☆ **The Blond Ambition World Tour shocked the world by exporting lewd American culture.** In the US, Madonna put on a sexy show, but it didn't raise opposition. However, when she took the same show outside of the US, cops were called and boycotts were staged. Madonna's tour was a confirmation that the overtly sexual and no-holds-barred pop culture of America was spreading elsewhere— and lots of places weren't happy.

☆ **The Blond Ambition World Tour inspired other female pop stars to use their sexuality as a selling point.** Though Madonna's fearless sexuality is what got her in trouble time after time, it also helped make her into the mega-star she is today. And aspiring female pop stars took note. You can still see her influence in the sexy clothes, grinding dance moves, and wild theatrical performances of Britney Spears, Christina Aguilera, and Lady Gaga, to name a few.

MORE SHOCKING MOMENTS FROM MADONNA

➡ *1984 MTV Video Music Awards (VMAs).* Madonna first caused a stir performing her hit "Like A Virgin" at the very first MTV VMAs. During her much talked-about performance, she came out of a huge (fake) wedding cake, and sang about feeling "shiny and new" while she crawled, rolled, and humped her way around the stage in a white, lacey wedding dress with a belt buckle that said Boy Toy.

➡ *1989 "Like A Prayer" Video.* This video contained a rape scene, a scantily clad Madonna parading around a church, and a field of burning crosses. Christian groups were offended, and Madonna lost an endorsement deal with Pepsi, but "Like A Prayer" became one of her biggest hits.

➡ *2003 MTV Video Music Awards (VMAs).* At the 20th annual MTV VMAs, reining pop stars Britney Spears and Christina Aguilera paid tribute to Madonna by singing "Like A Virgin" on top of a big wedding cake (just like the one she jumped out of in 1984). They wore their own lingerie-like wedding dresses and rolled and humped around the stage in homage. Then, Madonna herself popped out of the cake, dressed as a groom in a skin-tight tuxedo, singing one of her new hits. For added shock value, the pop star planted an open-mouthed kiss first on Britney, then on Christina.

THE SCOOP!

Supreme Court Nominee Clarence Thomas was accused of sexual harassment by a former employee resulting in highly publicized Senate hearings that put the spotlight on a rarely talked about crime.

WHAT WENT DOWN

It was October of 1991. Republican President George Bush had just nominated Clarence Thomas for a spot on the Supreme Court. Thomas, who is black, had been chosen to replace the very first (and only) black Supreme Court Justice, Thurgood Marshall, who was retiring. At the time, Thomas seemed to have a clean record. The most controversial thing about him was how politically conservative he was—but as a conservative Republican, Bush liked that. Liberal Democrats put up a fight, but it still looked like Thomas would grab a lifetime seat in the highest court in the country.

Then, two days before the Senate vote to confirm his appointment, an FBI report was leaked to the press with testimony from a former employee, Anita Hill, claiming Thomas had sexually harassed her. The report was actually old news to the (all male) Senate Judiciary Committee in charge of reviewing nominated judges. They'd read the report but didn't think the accusations were a big deal. Sexual harassment had only been against the law for five years, and many people (including some women) still didn't understand what it was and why it was wrong.

However, the few women who were serving in Congress made a stink about the charges against Thomas and convinced Congress to look into them before giving him the job.

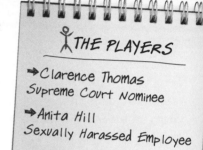

THE PLAYERS

➡ Clarence Thomas
Supreme Court Nominee

➡ Anita Hill
Sexually Harassed Employee

Clarence Thomas at the Senate Judiciary Committee hearing, 1991.

The three days of hearings that followed were televised live on all the major networks, and Hill and Thomas told very different stories. Hill testified that Thomas kept coming on to her while she worked for him at the Department of Education (DOE) and the Equal Employment Opportunity Commission (EEOC). (Ironically, the EEOC is in charge of enforcing laws against sexual harassment.)

According to Hill, Thomas repeatedly asked her out (she always said no), loved to brag about how awesome he was in bed (which made her squeamish), and enjoyed describing graphic scenes from his favorite porn movies.

QUOTEABLES

"Here is a person who is in charge of protecting rights of women and other groups in the workplace and he is using his position of power for personal gain for one thing. And he did it in a very ugly and intimidating way."

Anita Hill in an interview with NPR on October 6, 1991 (the day the FBI report was leaked to the press), explaining why she decided to come forward with her allegations of sexual harassment.

"[The hearings are a] circus, it's a national disgrace. It is a high-tech lynching for uppity blacks who in any way deign to think for themselves."

Clarence Thomas in his opening remarks during the Senate Judiciary Committee hearings on October 11, 1991.

Once he even joked to her about finding pubic hairs on his can of Coke. After being hospitalized for stress-related stomach pains, Hill said she'd had enough and quit her job to teach at Oral Roberts University. A number of people backed up Hill's story, including another female employee of Thomas' who said she wasn't bothered by it, but that was how he acted in the office.

Thomas denied everything. He compared the hearings to being lynched and accused Hill of playing on stereotypes of black men as sexual aggressors. He even implied that Hill was just jealous because she knew he preferred lighter-skinned black women. In the end, everyone involved in the hearings looked bad. While surveys showed that a majority of Americans sided with Thomas, his name would always be connected with sexual harassment. Hill was portrayed as an unstable woman who was paid off by shady liberals to ruin a powerful man's career. And the Judiciary Committee came off as a bunch of out-of-touch, over-privileged, old dudes out to protect one of their own. Thomas did finally get confirmed. In October of 1991, he became the 106th Supreme Court Justice in a 52–48 vote—the slimmest win in Supreme Court history.

THE AFTERMATH

Clarence Thomas: In 2007, Thomas released his autobiography, *My Grandfather's Son*, in which he angrily stands by his version of events. Then, in February of 2011, Lillian McEwan, a woman who dated him right before the hearings, went public in support of Hill claiming Thomas was a porn-obsessed binge drinker the whole time they were going out. She talked about this in her memoir, *DC Unmasked and Undressed*, which was released the same year. Thomas is still on the Supreme Court.

Anita Hill: After the trial, Hill taught law at the University of Oklahoma and later at Brandeis University in Boston. Most of her courses deal with racial and gender equality. She rarely speaks publicly, but in 1998 she released a memoir, *Speaking Truth to Power*, in which she talked about the hearings and the fallout afterward. In October of 2010, nearly 20 years after the hearings, Clarence Thomas' wife, Virginia, left a message on Hill's work voice mail demanding an apology for what Hill did to her husband. Hill never called back to apologize, and she continues to stand by her testimony.

WHY WE STILL CARE

☆ **The hearings put a necessary spotlight on sexual harassment.** Before Anita Hill came on to the scene, most people didn't really know what sexual harassment was or why it was a problem. Hill's actions inspired other women to come forward with complaints and over the next year, the number of reported cases of sexual harassment doubled. After the hearings, the first President Bush signed the Civil Rights Act of 1991, which let victims of sexual harassment sue for money. Since, employers are responsible for paying settlements in sexual harassment cases, no matter who does the harassing, most companies now conduct special training to prevent it.

☆ **The scandal encouraged more women to go into politics.** Women's groups felt that the all-male Judiciary Committee unfairly sided with Thomas, and many women took the hearings as a sign that more women were needed in politics. In the 1992 elections, the number of women in the Senate tripled from two to six and the number of women in the House of Representatives rose from 28 to 47.

MORE SUPREME COURT MISHAPS

➡ **1894 Wheeler Hazard Peckham and William B. Hornblower.** Congress is filled with all kinds of quirky rules like "Senatorial courtesy," which gives Senators the right to block any Supreme Court candidate that comes from his or her home state. For whatever reason, New York Senator David Hill decided to use his "courtesy" to do just that to New Yorkers Peckham and Hornblower, both of whom President Grover Cleveland tried to nominate in 1894.

➡ **1987 Robert Bork.** Republican President Ronald Reagan nominated super-conservative Republican Bork for the Supreme Court. But Democrats disliked Bork because he was pro death penalty and anti abortion, both of which go against most Democrats' views. The Democrats fought so hard against his nomination (and succeeded) that getting "Borked" became code for taking down a Supreme Court nominee based on his or her political views.

➡ **2005 Harriet Myers.** President George W. Bush's first choice to replace Sandra Day O'Connor on the Supreme Court was his own lawyer, White House counsel Harriet Myers. Many questioned whether Myers was qualified for the job; she was a lawyer but had never served as a judge or written about Constitutional law. It seemed the only thing she was really good at was her 20 years of loyal service to Bush. Democrats and Republicans fought the nomination, and Myers withdrew herself as a candidate before she could be rejected.

THE SCOOP!

African American LA resident Rodney King was pulled over for drunk driving by white police officers, and then beaten. The officers got off with no penalty—even though the beating was filmed—and LA became the scene of a violent and destructive riot.

WHAT WENT DOWN

In March of 1991, Los Angeles TV station KTLA received a shocking video taken the night before. It showed three white Los Angeles Police Department (LAPD) officers repeatedly beating an African American man, Rodney King, who they'd pulled over after a drunken chase. The home video shot by civilian on-looker George Holliday showed eleven more officers standing back and watching as King was hit with batons (56 times), kicked, and shocked with a stun gun. When the beating was over, the officers hog-tied King and left him on the side of the road until an ambulance came. When King was released from the hospital, the district attorney said there wasn't enough evidence to charge him with anything and he was set free. He was badly bruised; his leg, cheekbone, and eye socket were broken; his skull was fractured; and he was left with permanent nerve damage to his face.

The three officers involved in King's attack, along with their commanding officer, Stacey Koon (who shot King with a stun gun but didn't beat him), were charged with assault with a deadly weapon and excessive use of force. TV stations worldwide replayed the

☆ THE PLAYERS

➡ Rodney King
Assaulted Victim

➡ Daryl Gates
The LA Police Chief

➡ Lawrence Powell, Theodore Briseno, and Timothy Wind
Brutalizing Police Officers

➡ Stacey Koon
Officer in Charge

footage and viewers were horrified by the blatant police brutality. But for the African American community in LA, there was an upside—finally people would see how police had been treating them all these years. Everyone, including the mayor of LA, was calling for LA Police Chief Daryl Gates to step down, saying he was obviously doing something wrong if this happened on his watch. The mayor organized an investigation into police behavior, which found that this type of abuse happened frequently to minority suspects and usually went unpunished.

The officers caught a break when an LA Superior Court judge moved their trial out of LA, saying the public outrage in the city was too widespread for the men to get a fair trial. The trial was moved to a suburb outside LA that had almost no African American residents, but had lots of white law enforcement families who were sympathetic to the officers. During

A scene from the video of Los Angeles police officers beating Rodney King, 1991.

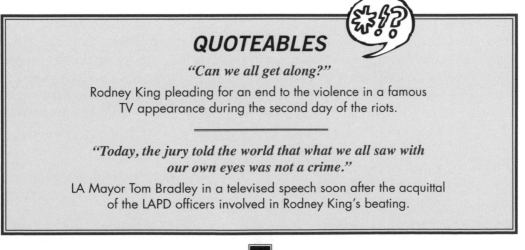

QUOTEABLES

"Can we all get along?"

Rodney King pleading for an end to the violence in a famous TV appearance during the second day of the riots.

"Today, the jury told the world that what we all saw with our own eyes was not a crime."

LA Mayor Tom Bradley in a televised speech soon after the acquittal of the LAPD officers involved in Rodney King's beating.

the trial in April of 1992, the police argued that King was drunk, threatening, and too strong to subdue without a beating. The jury agreed, and the officers were fully acquitted.

The verdict angered a lot of people. Hours later, in the mostly African American neighborhood of South Central LA, residents took their anger to the streets, sparking a riot that quickly spread throughout the city. Storefronts were smashed, looted, and burned to the ground. Even stores with signs saying "Black Owned" weren't spared from destruction. In an echo of the King beating, a video taken from a news helicopter showed Reginald Denny, a white truck driver, yanked from his truck and repeatedly hit with a hammer and a cinder block until his skull was crushed while a crowd cheered. The mayor declared a state of emergency and set a citywide curfew. President Bush called in 6,000 National Guard, Army, and Marine troops to control the violence, but massive damage was already done. After two days of rioting, more than 50 people were killed, more than 2,000 were injured, more than 7,000 arrests were made, and $1 billion in damage was done to the city.

THE AFTERMATH

The Police Officers: Soon after the riots, President Bush worked with the Attorney General to put the officers back on trial, this time on federal charges for violating King's civil rights. Unlike the first criminal trial, the second trial was held in LA, had a racially mixed jury, and included moving testimony from King himself. Commanding officer Stacey Koon and Lawrence Powell, the officer responsible for most of King's beating, were both found guilty and sentenced to 30 months in federal corrections camps. Theodore Briseno and Timothy Wind were found not guilty but were both fired from the LAPD soon after the federal trial.

Rodney King: King received a $3.8 million settlement from the city of Los Angeles. But his trouble with the law continued after the riots. He was arrested for a number of offenses, including beating his wife and more drunk driving, and was in and out of rehab for years. In 2008, his stint at the Pasadena Recovery Center was featured in season two of the reality show *Celebrity Rehab with Dr. Drew*. He said he got clean and ultimately forgave the officers who attacked him.

WHY WE STILL CARE

☆ **The scandal influenced other people to tape violent crimes.** The tape of the Rodney King beating was proof that police were brutalizing the black community, a situation that went unacknowledged and unpunished for years. Although the white officers were acquitted in the criminal trial, it showed the public that the best way for people—especially minorities—to prove they're being victimized and call attention to their plight is to catch it all on video (see Oscar Grant in the sidebar).

☆ **The scandal forced the LAPD to change their tune.** Police Chief Daryl Gates resigned under pressure from the King beating, but other big changes were made, too. Two thousand new LAPD officers were hired, making it possible to do community policing, where officers are assigned to specific neighborhoods so they can build relationships with the community. The new officers had more diversity training and were given martial arts training and pepper spray to restrain suspects, instead of just the metal batons used to subdue King.

MORE POLICE BEHAVING BRUTALLY

➡ **Kathryn Johnston.** Atlanta police were acting on a tip from an informant when they raided 92-year-old Johnston's house in 2006. Thinking robbers were trying to break in, Johnston shot once over the cops' heads through the door. They shot back, killing her. Investigators later discovered that the police raid was based on falsified documents. Even worse, one of the officers planted drugs in Johnston's house after she was killed to cover up their mistake. Four officers involved in the raid were sentenced to between four and ten years in prison.

➡ **Sean Bell.** Like many grooms-to-be, 23-year-old Bell spent the night before his wedding day at a strip club with his buddies. As Bell and two friends (all unarmed) left the Queens, NY, club, police officers sprayed them with bullets, killing Bell and injuring his friends. Police said they thought Bell was drunk and going to his car to get a gun to settle a fight. The judge bought the story and found the cops not guilty.

➡ **Oscar Grant.** A fight broke out on a public transportation platform in Oakland, CA, on New Year's Eve in 2009. Bystanders took cell-phone video of transit police breaking it up and caught officer Johannes Mehserle shooting 22-year-old Grant in the back while Grant lay on his stomach in handcuffs. Grant's death was replayed over and over on the news and led to a series of protests and riots in Oakland. Mehserle was convicted of involuntary manslaughter and sentenced to two years in jail.

THE SCOOP!

In 1993, a 13-year-old boy claimed pop superstar Michael Jackson had molested him. Although Jackson was never convicted, his bizarre behavior led many to believe the allegations, which later haunted his life and tarnished his career.

WHAT WENT DOWN

Michael Jackson lived in the public eye and on top of pop music charts since the age of five. But by the late 1980s, people were more interested in Jackson's increasing weirdness than in his musical genius. He had worked most of his life under the watchful (and some say abusive) eye of his disciplinarian father, so as an adult Jackson seemed to become obsessed with reclaiming his lost youth.

Channeling his inner Peter Pan, he bought a huge property in California and named it Neverland Ranch. The sprawling 3,000-acre property was every kid's dream, filled with amusement park rides, a video game arcade, and even a zoo. Outside the ranch, he hung out with an entourage of mostly underage boys and Bubbles, his pet chimpanzee. If refusing to grow up wasn't strange enough, Jackson was altering his image with plastic surgeries. He admitted to a nose job, but the changes to his appearance over time were so drastic, his face made more headlines than his music.

Amid all this bizarre (but seemingly harmless behavior), allegations began to surface in 1992 that Jackson had kissed, and sexually touched one of his young friends, 13-year-old Jordan Chandler. According to Jackson, Evan Chandler (Jordan's dad) tried to use his son's accusations of sexual molestation to blackmail Jackson for millions of dollars. But when Jackson

THE PLAYERS

→ Michael Jackson
(Eccentric) King of Pop

→ Jordan Chandler
Underage Accuser

→ Evan Chandler
Jordan's Money-Hungry Dad

refused to be blackmailed, Chandler made good on his threats by going to the police and the press.

There was no real proof to back up the Chandlers' story, but the media still had a field day with Jackson. Tabloids dubbed him "Wacko Jacko" and published scathing stories speculating on what he did with the kids he hung out with. Meanwhile, the state of California opened a criminal investigation against Jackson, and the Chandlers filed a civil lawsuit. Police searched Neverland Ranch for evidence and even got Jackson to agree to a strip search so they could check if his genitals matched up with Jordan's description. It wasn't a definitive match, but that didn't stop the public from presuming he was guilty.

Amid media attacks and a 13-month police probe, Jackson was never arrested and always maintained his innocence.

Michael Jackson at one of his later trials for child molestation.

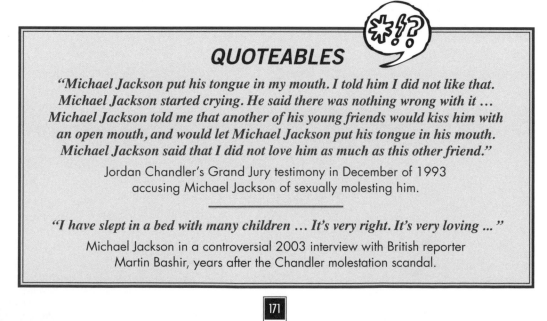

QUOTEABLES

"Michael Jackson put his tongue in my mouth. I told him I did not like that. Michael Jackson started crying. He said there was nothing wrong with it … Michael Jackson told me that another of his young friends would kiss him with an open mouth, and would let Michael Jackson put his tongue in his mouth. Michael Jackson said that I did not love him as much as this other friend."

Jordan Chandler's Grand Jury testimony in December of 1993 accusing Michael Jackson of sexually molesting him.

"I have slept in a bed with many children … It's very right. It's very loving ... "

Michael Jackson in a controversial 2003 interview with British reporter Martin Bashir, years after the Chandler molestation scandal.

In 1994, against his wishes Jackson's insurance company forked over a reported $20 million to the Chandler family to settle the civil case out of court. After the payout, Jordan suddenly refused to testify against his supposed attacker in criminal court, leading many to believe all the Chandlers wanted was the money. And all of the criminal charges were dropped.

Despite the Chandlers' shadiness and a lack of proof that Jackson committed a crime, the accusations of child molestation followed him for years. He didn't help his rep when he agreed to an exclusive interview with British reporter Martin Bashir in 2003. The interview was turned into a must-see TV event called *Living With Michael Jackson*, during which Jackson described sleeping in bed with other people's children as a "loving" act. Later that year, a boy who had appeared in the TV interview holding Jackson's hand accused the pop star of molestation. This time there was a trial and the press went wild reporting every weird detail, including Jackson's choice of wardrobe in court (pajamas!). However, once again, there wasn't much to the case and Jackson was acquitted on all charges.

THE AFTERMATH

Michael Jackson: Jackson never really recovered emotionally from the initial molestation scandal. The string of negative publicity caused him to turn to prescription pain killers. After the 2003 trial, Jackson disappeared with his three children—Prince, Paris, and Blanket Jackson—to live on the Middle Eastern island of Bahrain. In 2009, he announced a comeback tour but died tragically of an accidental drug overdose before he could restore his ruined rep. Despite the bad publicity that plagued Jackson's life, millions worldwide mourned his death. The week after he died, he had the top three bestselling albums in the US and was the top-grossing dead celebrity in 2010.

The Chandlers: After the payout, Jordan went to live with his father, Evan, who blamed his ex-wife for allowing Jackson too much access to their son. Evan, fearful of retribution from angry Jackson fans, had almost as much drastic plastic surgery as the pop star himself in an attempt to hide his identity. Father and son remained close until 2006, when Jordan accused his father of attacking him with a dumbbell and spraying him with mace, after which they became estranged. In 2010, Evan was found dead in his New Jersey apartment of a self-inflicted gunshot wound. He left no suicide note.

WHY WE STILL CARE

⭐ **The scandal is a great example of character assassination.** Michael Jackson lived an eccentric lifestyle, but there is still no proof that he ever did anything inappropriate with a kid. Regardless, many people were willing to believe the worst about him—and the media played a huge role in helping the public form its negative opinion of the pop star.

⭐ **The scandal showed the side-effects of young stardom.** Most people see Jackson's obsession with childhood as a side effect of missing out on his own. To be a successful child celebrity, you often have to replace play dates, school, and just plain fun with work. Sure, it seems like a great (and very profitable) idea at the time, but all that Hollywood pressure can cause a person to crack.

MORE CHILD STAR CASUALTIES

➡️ **Danny Bonaduce.** Bonaduce stole the show as a wisecracking red-headed kid on the 1970s show *The Partridge Family*. But when the show ended he found himself homeless and addicted to drugs. While he eventually started working again as a radio personality, he wasn't able to kick his habit. He was arrested a bunch of times for drug possession and once, in 1991, for assaulting a transvestite. In true TV fashion, he attempted suicide during the taping of his reality show *Breaking Bonaduce*. Since the suicide attempt, he's sobered up, hopefully for good.

➡️ **Jodie Sweetin.** While Sweetin's *Full House* co-stars Mary Kate and Ashley Olson were building their media empire, she was acquiring a nasty meth addiction. She married a cop in her early 20s, but even he couldn't keep her straight. She went to rehab but relapsed soon after, cleaning up once again to regain custody of her daughter. She shared all her struggles in her 2009 memoir, *unSweetined*.

➡️ **Lindsay Lohan.** LiLo started acting when she was just three years old, and by the late 1990s she'd starred in a slew of Disney films, including *The Parent Trap* and *Freaky Friday*. But her image wasn't so G-rated off screen, where she was partying at nightclubs, driving (and crashing) her car while drunk, getting caught with cocaine, going in and out of rehab, and even doing a short stint in prison. She's still trying to get it together.

THE SCOOP!

When the police heard that an isolated religious sect called the Branch Davidians was gathering tons of explosives in a compound in Waco, Texas, they sent firearms officials to check it out. The result was a 51-day siege that ended in a tragic mass death.

WHAT WENT DOWN

The Branch Davidians were a religious group who took the Bible very literally spending most of their time preparing for an upcoming apocalypse. They lived in a secluded cluster of cottages and buildings outside Waco, Texas. David Koresh, a high school dropout, born Vernon Howell, went to live with them after his dream of becoming a rock 'n' roll star didn't pan out. After just a few years on the compound, he became the sect's leader. He started calling himself the Messiah and said the best way to prep for the end of times was to cut off ties with the outside world and stockpile food and weapons.

Not all the Davidians were happy with Koresh. Some members started to defect and speak out against him. They told the local paper that while men in the compound were sworn to celibacy, Koresh took many of the women as "wives" (some barely in their teens). They also said Koresh was abusing the children in other ways. When local police learned about frequent shipments of firearms to the compound, they asked the Bureau of Alcohol, Tobacco, and Firearms (ATF) to help investigate the situation. On February 28, 1993, the ATF showed up at the compound with a search warrant. Unfortunately, someone had already tipped the Davidians off about the upcoming visit, and they were armed and ready.

THE PLAYERS

→David Koresh
Leader of the Branch Davidians

→Janet Reno
Attorney General

ATF agents claim the Davidians fired first, and the Davidians claim the ATF fired first. Whoever started it, the shootout ended with four dead ATF agents. Another 16 agents were wounded, along with Koresh and an unknown number of Davidians. Within hours, local police, the Texas Rangers, a bomb squad, and the FBI (who took charge) arrived to help the ATF. Inside the compound, Koresh and his followers, including 42 kids, locked their doors, drew their guns, and stood their ground. The compound remained under siege for the next 51 days.

During that time, hundreds of reporters flocked to the site, while hostage negotiators tried to convince Koresh to let them in, or at least let the kids out. Koresh did release 35 people, including 21 kids, but he also sent some very mixed messages. One day he promised to end the standoff if a tape of his religious ramblings was broadcast on TV. The tapes were played, but the standoff continued. Three days later, Koresh released a little girl

The Branch Davidian compound on fire, 1993.

QUOTEABLES

"I AM your God, and you will bow under my feet. Do you think you have the power to stop my will?"

David Koresh in a text message to FBI agents on the weekend of April 10, 1993.

"Obviously, if I had thought that the chances were great of a mass suicide, I would never have approved the plan."

Attorney General Janet Reno in an interview with the *New York Times*.

with a note pinned to her jacket that said once all the children were released, the adults would kill themselves. Frustrated and hoping to end the standoff, the FBI tried to put pressure on Koresh by shutting off the electricity on the compound, shining spotlights into the buildings all night, and blasting annoying music from loud speakers. Nothing worked, and Koresh continued to make and break promises.

As the siege dragged on, the FBI and Attorney General Janet Reno started to worry about the kids and the possibility of a mass suicide. Finally, Reno gave the FBI the go signal to use tear gas to flush Koresh and his followers out of the buildings. On the morning of April 19, the FBI began squirting tear gas into holes they'd drilled in the compound walls. The Davidians started shooting at them, but the FBI kept pumping the tear gas in. But the Davidians put on gas masks.

Six hours later, it was clear the tear gas plan was a bust. Then, things took a turn for the worst. Fires were set inside the compound, and more gunshots were heard. FBI agents yelled for everyone to run out and tried to put out the flames, but it was too windy and the fires spread too fast. When the chaos ended and all the bodies were counted, there were 75 Davidians dead—including 25 children and Koresh.

THE AFTERMATH

The Deaths: President Clinton ordered two separate investigations into the ATF and the FBI's actions—to find out how the deaths could have been avoided. The Treasury Department report blamed the ATF saying they should have called off the first raid when agents realized Koresh knew they were coming. The Justice Department report blamed Janet Reno and the FBI, saying they should have waited to see if negotiations with Koresh paid off before busting in with tear gas. Finally, an independent counsel report released in 2000 cleared the government of wrongdoing and blamed Koresh and the Davidians for firing the first shots and starting the deadly fires.

The Branch Davidians: David Koresh was buried in an unmarked grave, along with his first wife, Rachel, who also died during the siege, and 26 of his unclaimed or unidentified followers. Eleven Branch Davidians who survived the raid and siege were charged with murder, conspiracy, and possession of illegal weapons. Several were sentenced to prison time. The ruins of the compound still attract visitors and a reorganized sect of the Branch Davidians has built a chapel there.

☆ **The Waco raid changed how the FBI responds to crises.** While there were around 250 FBI agents at Waco, there was no cohesive plan. So although the court found that the FBI didn't do anything wrong, they didn't do anything right either. The big botch led to the creation of the Critical Incident Response Group in 1994. They take charge if there's a terrorist attack, natural disaster, prison riot, or, say, a religious group trapped in a compound sitting on tons of firepower.

☆ **Koresh and his followers inspired other radicals.** Janet Reno and the FBI couldn't have picked a less auspicious day to execute their raid on Waco. April 19 was already a well-known date among Americans who considered the federal government their enemy (see sidebar). But after the raid on Waco, April 19 officially became known as the "Date of Doom," and Waco became a call to action for other violent anti-government radicals.

MORE ANTIGOVERNMENT BATTLES THAT HAPPENED ON APRIL 19

➡ **The Battle of Lexington.** For Americans, the importance of April 19 goes way back to 1775, before we even were Americans. That was the day our colonist forefathers (aided by Paul Revere's famous ride the night before) fought, and won, the very first battle of the American Revolution.

➡ **The Siege of the Covenant, the Sword, and the Arm of the Lord (CSA).** This organization, with its unwieldy but colorful name, had a lot in common with the Branch Davidians. It was a small, heavily armed radical religious group living in a rural area that the ATF thought it'd better take a look at. The CSA got their own siege, too, on April 19, 1985. But unlike the Waco debacle, it only lasted four days and ended peacefully.

➡ **The Oklahoma Bombing.** Two years after the FBI raid on the Davidians' compound, Timothy McVeigh blew up a federal building in Oklahoma, killing 167 people and wounding 509 more. McVeigh considered the terrorist act, which took place on April 19, 1995, a tribute to the lives lost at Waco.

THE SCOOP!

When 27-year-old Heidi Fleiss was busted for running a multimillion-dollar Hollywood prostitution ring, the reputations of some of the richest and most powerful men in Los Angeles were suddenly at stake.

WHAT WENT DOWN

High school dropout Heidi Fleiss entered the world's oldest profession in 1988 when she met Elizabeth "Madam Alex" Adams, a 60-year-old immigrant from the Philippines, at a Hollywood party. At the time, Madam Alex ran Los Angeles' most successful prostitution ring. Fleiss started working for her as a prostitute when she was 22, but soon she was running the organization. Fleiss brought in new, younger, better-looking workers, and profits increased by a whopping 400 percent. But Madam Alex only paid Fleiss a tiny fraction of the money she was bringing in.

So, two years after she started working for Madam Alex, Fleiss struck out on her own. According to Fleiss, it only took four months to earn her first million dollars as the head of her own call girl ring. Her client list was full of the richest and most powerful men in Hollywood: actors, studio heads, producers, and other assorted international millionaires and billionaires. For two-and-a-half years, Fleiss dominated the high end of the LA call girl market and partied with celebrities, many of whom were her clients.

Then she got busted. In 1993, an FBI agent posing as a Hawaiian businessman made a deal with Fleiss to send four prostitutes and

THE PLAYERS

→ Heidi Fleiss
Hollywood Madam

→ Madam Alex
Original Madam

13 grams of cocaine to a Beverly Hills hotel room. She did, and the next day Fleiss was arrested outside her house while taking out the trash. Fleiss has long blamed her competitors for leaking information to the police out of professional jealousy.

It's not unusual for a madam to get arrested. What made Fleiss unusual was that because her business serviced so many famous men, she had a lot of information the media was dying to get a hold of. Though several of her clients were found out by the police, many remained a secret, causing rumors to fly. If Fleiss leaked any

Hollywood madam Heidi Fleiss lounging on a bed, 1995.

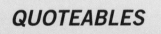

QUOTEABLES

"I took the oldest profession on Earth and I did it better than anyone on Earth. Alexander the Great conquered the world at 32. I conquered it at 22."

Heidi Fleiss in a 2005 TV interview with CNN.

"I made so many enemies, it was inevitable I would be arrested at some time, but who knew it would be such a mess. I didn't think it would be 10 years basically out of my life."

Heidi Fleiss in a 2002 interview on *Larry King Live* about her arrest in 1993 and the 10 years it took to get all of her legal problems behind her.

information to the press about her famous clients, she could ruin a lot of reputations. Fleiss, now known as The Hollywood Madam, never did release her clients' names to the press. She threatened at one point to write a tell-all book, but she has kept their secret to this day.

She did, however, go to jail. She was charged not only with pandering (setting up an exchange of sex for money) and selling cocaine, but tax fraud, too. Since her business was illegal, she never reported her income to the IRS. Fleiss pled guilty to attempted pandering and was found guilty of conspiracy, income tax evasion, and money laundering. She was sentenced to 37 months in a California prison, but only served 20.

THE AFTERMATH

Heidi Fleiss: After her release from prison in 1998, Fleiss wrote a memoir called *Pandering* and released an instructional video, *Sex Tips with Heidi Fleiss and Victoria Sellers*. She later moved to the Nevada desert where she lived with 24 parrots, struggled with substance abuse, and opened a coin-op laundromat called Dirty Laundry. She has also appeared on the dating show *Blind Date* and on the reality shows *Celebrity Big Brother, Celebrity Rehab with Dr. Drew*, and *Sober House*.

The Celebrities: To her clients' relief and the public's disappointment, Fleiss kept her client list confidential. A few famous clients were revealed in other ways. Actor Charlie Sheen was forced to testify against her at the trial after police found checks he had written for her services.

WHY WE STILL CARE

☆ **The scandal showed the sexism inherent in prostitution laws.** While Fleiss was on trial for state and federal charges, the men who were identified as her clients were never charged with anything. The LA chapter of the National Organization of Women (NOW) demanded that police pursue arrests for her johns, but since pandering (what she did) is a felony and paying for sex (what the men did) is only a misdemeanor the police didn't bother going after the men. The laws remain unchanged.

☆ **Heidi Fleiss was one of the first celebrity society girls.** Despite the fact that she was breaking the law just by showing up for work, Fleiss refused to stay out of the spotlight. She threw parties full of celebrities and, simply by associating with famous people, became a celebrity herself. She set the stage for modern celebutantes like Paris Hilton and Kim Kardashian, whose fame revolve around partying with celebs and being rich.

MORE FAMOUS AMERICAN MADAMS

➡ ***The Mayflower Madam.*** Sydney Biddle Barrows, a socialite whose family was supposedly descended from the Pilgrims, ran a high-class call girl business in Manhattan in the 1980s. She even sent her girls out to jobs with credit card machines. Her bust in 1984 was front-page news every day, and the public eagerly awaited the release of her client list. But like Fleiss, Barrows' clients remained a secret. She pled guilty to promoting prostitution, paid a $5,000 fine, and, in return, got to keep all the money she earned.

➡ ***Madam Alex.*** Before Heidi Fleiss ran LA's most prestigious call girl ring, Madam Alex was in charge of hooking up Hollywood's richest men with beautiful women—for a price, of course. Though she pimped for almost 20 years, she kept out of jail by acting as an informant for the police. When she finally got busted in 1988, she only got probation—a much better deal than Fleiss'.

➡ ***Manhattan Madam.*** Kristin Davis became known as the Manhattan Madam after her high-class hooker ring entered the spotlight when news leaked in 2008 that New York Governor Elliot Spitzer was a customer. Although Spitzer's sexual escapades made headlines worldwide and he had to resign as governor, he faced no criminal charges. Meanwhile, Davis was convicted of promoting prostitution and spent four months behind bars.

THE SCOOP!

The world saw just how cutthroat competitive figure skating could get when figure skater Nancy Kerrigan was clubbed in the knee just before the 1994 Olympics by the ex-husband of rival figure skater Tonya Harding.

WHAT WENT DOWN

In the world of figure skating, a win at the United States Figure Skating Association (USFSA) Championships is the first step toward an Olympic medal. In 1994, the top contenders were figure skaters Nancy Kerrigan (America's sweetheart) from Plymouth, Massachusetts, and Tonya Harding (Kerrigan's tough-girl archrival) from Portland, Oregon.

Two days before the USFSA, a man clubbed Kerrigan's right knee with a metal baton in a surprise attack as she was leaving the rink. The injury forced her to withdraw from the competition, though she was back on the ice within weeks. Harding easily skated her way to first place and secured herself a spot on the Olympic team. Even though she couldn't compete, Kerrigan was allowed to join the Olympic team, too. USFSA bigwigs wanted her on the team so badly they scoured the rulebooks until they found a loophole saying they could put a skater on the Olympic team even if she hadn't competed in the most recent Nationals.

☆THE PLAYERS

➤ **Tonya Harding**
Disgruntled Figure Skater

➤ **Nancy Kerrigan**
Favored Skater and Attack Victim

➤ **Jeff Gillooly**
Attack Planner and Harding's Ex-Husband

➤ **Shawn Eckardt**
Attack Planner #2 and Harding's Bodyguard

➤ **Shane Stant**
Knee Whacker

➤ **Derrick Smith**
Getaway Car Driver

At first, the attack seemed like the work of an unhinged fan. But within a week, the FBI was investigating Harding's ex-husband, Jeff Gillooly (who she was living with at the time), along with Harding's bodyguard, Shawn Eckardt. The motive was obvious: Kerrigan was Harding's toughest competition in the 1994 Championships. Plus, Kerrigan had beat Harding out for the Bronze medal at the 1992 Winter Olympics in Albertville, France, sending Harding home empty-handed.

Eckardt confessed right away to his part in planning the attack. He also implicated Harding and Gillooly as co-conspirators and told the FBI that two of his thug buddies, Shane Stant (the knee whacker) and Derrick Smith (the getaway-car driver), were hired to carry out the actual attack. Gillooly and the thugs turned themselves in, but Harding continued

Tonya Harding and Nancy Kerrigan during practice for the 1994 Winter Olympics.

to deny any role in the attack though many found this hard to believe. Then, during a pre-Olympics press conference three weeks later, she tearfully admitted she found out

QUOTEABLES

"Let me tell you, I'm going to go there and kick some butt."

Tonya Harding to reporters at the Portland International Airport in January of 1994 while on her way to USFSA Championships in Detroit, where the attacks took place.

"Why me? Why now? Help me! Help me!"

Nancy Kerrigan's tearful question, caught on camera immediately after the attack on her knee on January 6, 1994.

after the attack that Gillooly and Eckhart were involved, and she helped them cover things up by lying to the police, but wasn't in on the plan.

As the scandal unfolded, figure skating officials had to decide if they were going to let Harding compete in the Olympics, which were coming up fast. They tried to get Harding to withdraw, but she refused. When they tried to hold hearings to investigate her part in the attack, she filed a $20 million lawsuit to stop them. Tired of the drama, officials announced she'd be on the team but warned they'd resume the investigation after the Olympics.

The press took full advantage of the ongoing controversy, turning the 1994 Lillehammer Olympics into a Harding vs. Kerrigan battle royale. Hundreds of reporters and photographers descended to watch the skaters' first practice on the rink together, and all of them were psyched to see Kerrigan wearing the same outfit she was attacked in. In addition, the primetime games became one of the top ten most watched network broadcasts of all time with 48 million viewers. Kerrigan went on to win the Silver medal in individual women's figure skating, while Harding came in at a disappointing eighth place.

THE AFTERMATH

Tonya Harding: Harding copped to "conspiracy to hinder an investigation," for her role in the cover-up and got 500 hours of community service and a $100,000 fine. She was stripped of her 1994 USFSA Championship title and was forced to resign from the USFSA, ending her skating career. In the years to follow, a sex tape of her and Gillooly was released to the press, she was arrested for driving drunk, and she spent three days in jail for attacking a boyfriend with a hubcap.

Nancy Kerrigan: After winning the Silver medal at the Olympics, Kerrigan was more popular than ever. She graced the covers of magazines like *Time* and *People*, was a guest host on *Saturday Night Live*, and starred in a parade at Disney World, her new multi-million dollar sponsor. But she didn't compete again in the Olympics. She did, however, appear in a cameo in Will Ferrell's 2007 skating movie *Blades of Glory*, and she became a special correspondent for *Entertainment Tonight* in 2010.

The Attackers: Stant, Smith, Eckhardt, and Gillooly all served time in prison. After being released from jail, both Gillooly and Eckhardt changed their names to distance themselves from the scandal.

WHY WE STILL CARE

☆ **Tonya Harding has come to symbolize winning at all costs.** Since the scandal, Harding has become a colorful symbol for taking out the competition by any means necessary—including violence. During the Democratic primaries for the 2008 presidential election, strategists claimed that Obama's only way to win was to pull a Harding and use vicious tactics against the person ahead of him. He publicly insisted, however, on running a positive campaign, and not stooping to dirty tricks.

☆ **The scandal made figure skating a more watched event.** Before the scandal, figure skating was generally seen as unexciting TV. It was just a bunch of people gliding around the ice in brightly colored spandex to classical music. But the scandal showed that skaters were serious athletes who would do anything for glory, and skating viewership increased. Since then, the TV ratings of figure skating competitions have depended on how compelling a front-running skater's storyline is.

MORE HARDING EXPLOITS

➡ **1995.** To put the skating scandal behind her, Harding made the next obvious career move—pop stardom. Unfortunately, singing didn't come as easily as skating. Harding and her band, The Golden Blades, had to run off stage during their first show because the audience wouldn't stop throwing bottles and yelling insults.

➡ **2002.** Harding appeared on the Fox show *Celebrity Boxing*, squaring off against Paula Jones, a woman who filed a sexual harassment suit against former President Bill Clinton (page 194). Harding dominated the match, even hitting Jones in the back of the head after she begged to end the fight.

➡ **2003.** Harding enjoyed punching pseudo celebrities so much, she decided to make a career out of boxing. She had her first professional fight in February 2003, but only competed in the ring for a year and a half ending with a record of three wins and three losses.

➡ **2008.** Harding's most recent gig has been as one of the commentators of the show *The Smoking Gun Presents: World's Dumbest*, which features real-life videos of people doing really idiotic things. Harding's co-hosts include a number of Hollywood has-beens, like Danny Bonaduce (page 173).

THE SCOOP!

Famous football player and movie star OJ Simpson was accused of brutally murdering his ex-wife and her friend; later he took off on a low-speed chase that ended in his arrest and a long, historic trial.

WHAT WENT DOWN

In June 12, 1994, the bodies of Nicole Brown and her friend Ron Goldman were found in a pool of blood in front of Brown's Brentwood, California, condo. Both had been viciously stabbed—Brown was almost decapitated. While the murders were gruesome, what really made it news was that beautiful, blonde-haired Brown was recently divorced from Football Hall of Famer and movie star OJ Simpson. While the public found it hard to believe that Simpson could ever commit such a horrific act, within days of the murders, evidence—including blood found at the scene of the crime—pointed to Simpson as the prime suspect. Simpson's lawyers worked out a deal that allowed Simpson to surrender to the LAPD quietly to prevent an embarrassing public arrest. But, on the morning he was supposed to give himself up, Simpson left the house of a friend and bolted in a white Ford Bronco with another friend, leaving behind what looked like a suicide note. The Bronco was eventually spotted on the highway and police followed it while cautiously negotiating over the phone with Simpson who was riding in the passenger seat with a gun to his head. The hour-long low-speed chase was broadcast live nationwide via a swarm of hovering news helicopters. Crowds

THE PLAYERS

→ OJ Simpson
Football Great Turned Murder Suspect

→ Nicole Brown Simpson
Murder Victim #1
(and OJ's Ex-Wife)

→ Ron Goldman
Murder Victim #2

gathered along the highway to cheer the passing Bronco, and 95 million viewers breathlessly watched as the Bronco pulled up to Simpson's house, where he was cuffed and arrested.

The highly publicized trial that followed lasted 252 days (the longest in LA history), making instant celebrities out of everyone involved. The prosecution accused Simpson of having committed the murder out of jealousy (Goldman was only a friend, but Simpson didn't know that) and called a parade of witnesses to the stand to testify that Simpson had been abusing Brown. They even played a chilling 911 phone call Brown made in 1989 while Simpson was attacking her. They also presented circumstantial evidence including a bloody glove found at Simpon's house that matched a glove found at Brown's.

OJ Simpson's mug shot after being arrested in 1994.

Simpson's defense team (the "Dream Team") was comprised of eight of the country's most famous attorneys. They argued that Simpson was another black man framed by racist cops who had planted evidence. It had only been

QUOTEABLES

"Don't feel sorry for me. I've had a great life, great friends. Please think of the real OJ and not this lost person."

OJ Simpson in the supposed suicide note he left behind before going on the lam in his white Bronco.

"The scariest homicides are always the ones where the bad guy is handsome, charming, someone who doesn't look like a murderer."

Prosecutor Marcia Clark in her closing statement during the OJ Simpson murder trial.

two years since Los Angeles Police Department (LAPD) officers had beaten Rodney King (page 166) and many still saw the LAPD as racist. The defense even dug up and played old audiotapes of Mark Fuhrman, the detective who found the bloody glove outside Simpson's house, using the "N" word over 50 times while discussing how he and other officers would sometimes plant evidence to help get convictions.

In the most theatrical moment of the trial, the prosecution had Simpson try on the aforementioned bloody glove. After Simpson struggled to pull on the glove, his lawyer Johnny Cochran famously cried, "If it doesn't fit, you must acquit!" The defense's forensic expert also poked holes in the prosecution's DNA evidence. Despite the long, drawn out case, in October of 1995, the jury spent only three hours deliberating Simpson's guilt, and 150 million people watched live as they finally delivered their verdict: Not guilty. The news divided the country. Many white people thought Simpson had gotten away with murder, while many black people saw the verdict as a triumph over racism.

THE AFTERMATH

OJ Simpson: A year after his victory in the criminal trial, Simpson was sued by the familes of Brown and Goldman for wrongful death. This was a civil trial, and so the prosecution only needed to prove that there was more than a 50 percent chance that the defendant did it. Simpson was found responsible for both deaths and ordered to pay a total of $33.5 million in damages. Then, in 2007, Simpson and some buddies robbed a sports memorabilia dealer, claiming they were retrieving some of Simpson's stolen memorabilia. He was arrested soon after and sentenced to 33 years behind bars for armed robbery.

The Murder: In 2006, book publisher Harper-Collins announced that it was going to release a book by Simpson called *If I Did It*, which would explain the way he would have murdered Brown and Goldman if he did it—which he still claimed he didn't. It was going to be accompanied by an interview on Fox News. But audiences didn't want to see Simpson make millions off of the murder, so both the interview and the book's publication were cancelled. In a weird twist, a civil court awarded the rights of the manuscript to Goldman's family, who added commentary and published it in 2007 under the name *If I Did It: Confessions of the Killer*. It instantly became a best seller.

☆ **The scandal showed a racially divided America.** Probably the most shocking thing about the Simpson trial was the reaction. On one side were disappointed white people who thought Simpson had gotten away with murder, and on the other joyful African Americans celebrating one of their own triumphing over a corrupt and racist system. It was a wake-up call for a country that prided itself on having overcome its color issues.

☆ **The scandal put the spotlight on domestic violence.** The police responded to eight domestic violence calls at the Simpson–Brown house before taking Simpson into custody in 1989 for assaulting his wife. At that time, police found Brown cowering in the bushes in her bra with a Simpson-size handprint on her throat and a bruised, bloodied, and swollen face. But all Simpson got as punishment was community service and a $700 fine. During the criminal trial, the jury didn't see a direct connection between the years of abuse and Brown's brutal murder, but after the trial, Brown became a symbol of the seriousness of domestic abuse in the US.

MORE TROUBLE BETWEEN CELEBRITY EXES

➡ **Paul McCartney and Heather Mills.** Former Beatle (McCartney) and former model (Mills) were married for just four years before they announced their split in 2006. Before long, they were trading accusations—McCartney said Mills was a gold digger, and Mills claimed that McCartney was abusive. After a vicious two-year court battle, Mills was awarded a $48.6 million settlement, one of the highest divorce settlements in history, but far less than the $250 million that Mills was asking for.

➡ **Alec Baldwin and Kim Basinger.** After seven years of marriage, actors Baldwin and Basinger announced their separation in 2001. The former couple lived on opposite coasts, and Baldwin complained that he didn't get enough time with their daughter. In 2007, a shocking voicemail message left by Baldwin for his daughter was leaked to the gossip website TMZ. In the recording, Baldwin called his daughter a "rude, thoughtless pig," and Basinger a "thoughtless pain in the ass."

➡ **Christie Brinkley and Peter Cook.** Supermodel Brinkley was married to architect Cook for 12 years. But then he slept with his 18-year-old "assistant." An irate Brinkley insisted the court records for their divorce be made public so the world could know that Cook spent $3,000 a month on porn and had tried to keep his young mistress quiet with $300,000 in hush money. After a two-year saga, Brinkley got full custody of the couple's two kids and almost all of the couple's assets.

THE SCOOP!

In the 1990s, Tupac Shakur and Biggie Smalls were two of hip hop's rising stars, but they were also two of the most public faces of the East Coast–West Coast rap rivalry. Their unsolved murders (which happened only six months apart) were a blow to the music world and changed the hip hop culture forever.

WHAT WENT DOWN

Rap star Tupac Shakur spent most of his childhood on the East Coast, but based his rap career out of California. He was signed to Death Row Records in LA, run by ex-convict Marion "Suge" Knight. Biggie Smalls (a.k.a. Notorious B.I.G.) was from New York and signed to Bad Boy Records, run by Sean "Diddy" Combs. During the 1990s, there was an ongoing rivalry between the East and West Coast rap worlds over whose rappers were better. Rappers representing their respective coasts exchanged insults via their music (also known as "diss tracks"). Hip hop fans took sides and, unfortunately, so did LA's inner-city gangs. The Mob Piru Bloods supported Death Row, while the Southside Crips supported Bad Boy. Despite the coastal feud, Tupac and Biggie remained friends. But that changed in 1994.

On November 30, 1994, Biggie and Tupac were both recording tracks at Quad Studio in New York City when Tupac and his entourage were ambushed in the lobby and robbed at gunpoint. Tupac was shot five times, including once in the head, but he miraculously survived

✶ THE PLAYERS

➡ Tupac Shakur
Death Row West Coast Rapper

➡ Biggie Smalls
Bad Boy East Coast Rapper

➡ Marion "Suge" Knight
President of Death Row Records

➡ Sean "Diddy" Combs
President of Bad Boy Records

without any serious injuries. The gunman did take off with around $40,000 worth of jewelry that Tupac was wearing at the time. Biggie repeatedly denied having anything to do with the shooting, but Tupac became convinced Biggie and Diddy set him up.

Two months after the shooting, Biggie released the song "Who Shot Ya" as a B-side to his hit debut album Ready To Die. The song was recorded before the shooting, but Tupac saw it as a diss track in which Biggie mocked the shooting and even took credit for it. As a comeback to Biggie's track, Tupac released the single "Hit 'Em Up" a few months later. In it, he alludes to Biggie's involvement in the shooting and talks about violently taking down the Bad Boy Rappers. The all-out lyric war heated up the East Coast–West Coast rivalry, resulting in a series of violent attacks from both sides.

Biggie and Tupac before their murders.

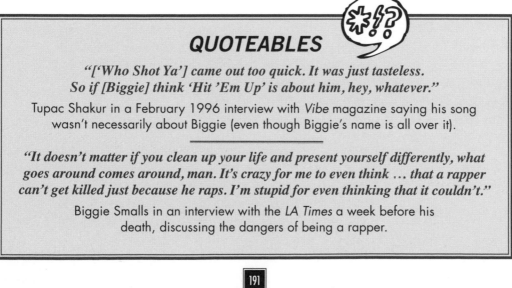

QUOTEABLES

"['Who Shot Ya'] came out too quick. It was just tasteless. So if [Biggie] think 'Hit 'Em Up' is about him, hey, whatever."

Tupac Shakur in a February 1996 interview with Vibe magazine saying his song wasn't necessarily about Biggie (even though Biggie's name is all over it).

"It doesn't matter if you clean up your life and present yourself differently, what goes around comes around, man. It's crazy for me to even think … that a rapper can't get killed just because he raps. I'm stupid for even thinking that it couldn't."

Biggie Smalls in an interview with the LA Times a week before his death, discussing the dangers of being a rapper.

On September 7, 1996, Tupac and Suge were in Las Vegas for the Tyson vs. Seldon match at the MGM Grand. After the match, Tupac and his entourage were caught on hotel security cameras beating and kicking a man in the lobby. According to later reports, one of Tupac's bodyguards recognized the man as part of a mob of Crips who had beat and robbed him of a gold Death Row necklace in a Foot Locker a month earlier. They left the man in the lobby and fled in a convoy of cars. While Tupac's car was stopped at a traffic light, a white Cadillac pulled up next to it, and someone inside fired at Tupac, hitting him three times. He was rushed to the hospital but died six days later. He was only 25 years old.

Because of the rivalry, many people believed Biggie was involved in Tupac's murder, but he denied having anything to do with it and insisted he was recording in New York on the night of the Vegas shooting. But that didn't stop the rumors. Then, just six months later, on March 9, 1997, Biggie was murdered, too. He was in LA to promote his new album and present an award at the Soul Train Awards. While Biggie's car was stopped at a red light (just like Tupac's), a man in a white Chevy Impala pulled up next to it and shot Biggie in the chest. He was only 24 years old.

THE AFTERMATH

The Murders: The murders remain unsolved and there is no real evidence that the deaths are connected. *Biggie and Tupac,* a documentary about the murders, was released in 2002, and *Notorious,* a movie about Biggie's life, was released in 2009.

Tupac Shakur: The album released after Tupac's death, The Don Killuminati: The Seven Day Theory, went platinum five times. After that, Death Row Records released ten more Tupac albums, making him the best-selling hip hop artist of all time. Tupac's song

"Dear Mama" was added to the Library of Congress's permanent collection, and the University of California Berkeley even ran a class on the works of Tupac in 2007.

Biggie Smalls: The album Biggie was promoting in LA when he was killed, ironically named Life After Death, went platinum 10 times after his murder. In 2002, he (along with Tupac) was among the first rappers to be inducted into the Hip Hop Hall of Fame. Biggie's family has always believed that the LAPD was somehow involved in his murder and have filed two lawsuits against the city of LA.

WHY WE STILL CARE

☆ **Biggie and Tupac's murders were a wake-up call to the hip hop community to end the smack talk.** In the 1990s, lots of rap music glorified violence, and lots of rap musicians publicly threatened each other. But the loss of two of hip hop's biggest stars showed a tragic downside to the hype. After Tupac's death, Russell Simmons, co-founder of the hip hop label Def Jam, hosted the first Hip Hop Summit. It called together rival rappers from both coasts to start a cease fire. After the second Hip Hop Summit in 2001, Simmons created the Hip Hop Summit Action Network. Its mission is to use hip hop to empower youth and advocate for civil rights and positive social change.

☆ **The scandal showed that being a rap star wasn't protection from the dangers of the street.** Hip hop is still one of the few legal routes for kids growing up in poverty to make it big. But that fame can come with a price. The murders of Tupac and Biggie showed that while rap could turn a poor kid from the ghetto into a star, it wasn't necessarily safer than life on the streets.

MORE UNSOLVED HIP HOP MURDERS

➡ ***Scott La Rock.*** Half of the hip hop duo Boogie Down Productions, La Rock was shot in the head in 1987 while sitting in a parked car with friends by an unknown gunman in an apartment building across the street. His Boogie Down Productions partner, rapper KRS-One, started the Stop the Violence Movement, which brought together rappers to speak out against the violence in the hip hop community.

➡ ***Jam Master Jay.*** Hip hop pioneer Run DMC was together for almost 20 years and was the first rap group to win a Grammy. The group had a rep for never getting caught up in feuds between other rappers, so people were shocked when its DJ, Jam Master Jay, was shot and killed inside a Queens, New York, recording studio in 2002. The hip hop world was rocked by the sudden loss of a founding father. The identity of the killer and the motive for the murder still remain a mystery.

➡ ***Mac Dre.*** San Francisco Bay Area rapper and leader of the Hyphy movement Mac Dre was in Kansas City for a performance in November 2004. While he and a friend were driving down the highway at 3:30 am another car pulled up next to them and shot into their van killing Mac Dre. Though police never found the rapper's killer, they believe the murder was related to a West Coast–Midwest rap rivalry.

THE SCOOP!

Democratic President Bill Clinton was leading the country through its longest period of peace and economic growth when he almost got kicked out of the White House for an affair with a 22-year-old intern.

WHAT WENT DOWN

Monica Lewinsky was a White House intern during President Clinton's first presidential term in 1995 and quickly became a paid employee within the year. But she was transferred to the Pentagon in 1996 because supervisors thought she was spending an inappropriate amount of time in the Oval Office (the office of the Prez). Meanwhile, President Clinton was under fire from Republicans and Independent Counsel Ken Starr, a lawyer whose job it was to keep the president in check. Neither the Republicans nor Starr liked Clinton's politics and they were trying to find evidence that he had done something wrong.

Throughout Clinton's presidency, Starr investigated many of his personal, political, and business dealings, including a lawsuit filed in 1994 by Paula Jones, a former employee who accused Clinton of sexual harassment during the time he was Governor of Arkansas (though she didn't sue him until he was president). During the Jones trial, the President was questioned about his relationship with Lewinsky. Under oath, he repeatedly denied ever having an affair with her, and Lewinsky did the same. Despite all of Starr's investigations, he couldn't get anything on the

☀THE PLAYERS

➡ Bill Clinton
Unfaithful President

➡ Monica Lewinsky
White House Intern

➡ Linda Tripp
Not-So-Loyal Co-Worker

➡ Ken Starr
Lawyer With a Mission

➡ Paula Jones
Clinton's Former Employee

White House photo of President Clinton with his intern, Monica Lewinsky, 1995.

President—until a woman named Linda Tripp handed Starr some interesting tapes.

Tripp had become friends with Lewinsky after she was transferred to the Pentagon. The tapes were phone conversations between the two women Tripp had secretly recorded. On the tapes, an unsuspecting Lewinsky spilled explicit details about a sexual affair she'd had with the President, talking about the times they'd had oral sex and even mentioning an incident where the president ruined one of her dresses by ejaculating on it. Tripp convinced Lewinsky not to dry clean the ruined dress or get rid of gifts Clinton had given her, in hopes that the items could all be used against him. Why Tripp did all of this still isn't totally clear; we do know that she was a loyal Republican, so the reason could have been political. (Some also say

QUOTEABLES

"I did not have sexual relations with that woman, Miss Lewinsky."

President Bill Clinton in a televised statement January 26, 1998, denying having had an inappropriate relationship with Monica Lewinsky.

"I did have a relationship with Miss Lewinsky that was not appropriate. In fact, it was wrong. It constituted a critical lapse in judgment and a personal failure on my part for which I am solely and completely responsible."

President Bill Clinton admitting to the affair seven months later in a live, prime-time televised event at the end of August 1998.

she was planning to write a book about the situation, though she never did.)

With the tapes, Starr could prove the President had lied under oath (perjury), which is against the law. Starr threatened Lewinsky with charges of perjury, in order to strike a deal; if she handed over the dress and agreed to testify against Clinton she wouldn't be charged with anything. With Lewinsky in his corner, Starr had some real proof that Clinton had committed perjury and tried to hide his lies (obstruction of justice). Starr mounted a $70 million investigation of the president, during which he famously defended himself by claiming he hadn't understood that oral sex was considered "sexual relations," and therefore hadn't lied. The 453-page report from the investigation, which detailed Clinton's sexual misdeeds in pornographic detail, became very popular on the internet. Based on the report, Clinton was impeached—put on trial to see if he should be allowed to stay president—for perjury and obstruction of justice. Fortunately for him, there weren't enough votes against him, and he stayed in office.

THE AFTERMATH

President Clinton: The saga didn't end after the impeachment trials. Two months later, the judge in the Paula Jones trial brought contempt of court charges against Clinton for lying about his relationship with Lewinsky during the sexual harassment trial. He was fined $90,000, and his license to practice law in Arkansas was suspended. He was never found guilty of sexual harassment but settled out of court with Jones for $850,000. After his presidency, Clinton published a memoir, *My Life*, and has devoted his time to various public policy campaigns. Clinton's wife, Hillary, served as a New York State Senator and ran for president in 2008.

She lost the Democratic nomination to Barack Obama but was named his Secretary of State after he took office. Bill Clinton was a huge supporter of his wife's political ambitions, and some say his guilt from the past had something to do with it.

Monical Lewinsky: In 1999, Lewinsky authorized Andrew Morton to write a biography of her side of the scandal called *Monica's Story*. She also launched a line of handbags and hosted a short running dating show called *Mr. Personality*. In 2006, she graduated from the London School of Economics with a master's degree in social psychology.

WHY WE STILL CARE

☆ **The scandal put a spotlight on the moral character of politicians.** Before the Clinton scandal, news about politicians focused mainly on their political decisions. But after the Clinton scandal, politicians' personal lives and religious beliefs made headlines. The public wanted to know that their leaders were not only making good political decisions, but also making good personal ones. A politician's moral character—how a politician lived his or her life—became increasingly important in elections and, as a result, Christian and Evangelical factions gained increasing influence on politics.

☆ **The Lewinsky scandal was one of the first stories to appear on the internet before it spread to traditional media like television and newspapers.** The story first "broke" on the online Drudge Report, and then appeared in print. This started a trend of stories breaking on the internet, which today is common.

MORE US IMPEACHMENT PROCEEDINGS

➡ ***10th President John Tyler*** was almost impeached by his own party (the Whigs) in 1841 for disagreeing with them on two key bills, but there weren't enough votes in the House of Representatives to go through with it.

➡ ***17th President Andrew Johnson,*** who became president after Lincoln was assassinated, was impeached in 1865 for firing his Secretary of State without the approval of the Senate. However, it really had more to do with disagreements with Republicans over how to bring the South back into the Union after the Civil War. He was spared from being kicked out of office by one single vote.

➡ ***37th President Richard Nixon*** was almost impeached in 1974 for Watergate (see page 110), but he resigned from office to avoid the impeachment trial.

THE SCOOP!

For the past 200 years, people have been gossiping about Thomas Jefferson's possible relationship with one of his female slaves, Sally Hemings. Finally, there was a DNA test that put the truth to rest. Or did it?

WHAT WENT DOWN

Thomas Jefferson helped found our country, wrote the Declaration of Independence, and was our third President, but rumors about his personal life have circulated for 200 years questioning his integrity. He lived during a time when slavery was common practice and spoke out against it, though he still owned approximately 200 slaves of his own. Most historians believed that after his young wife, Martha, died, he stayed so devoted to her memory that he focused only on his political career and never looked at another woman.

But there has also been a longstanding rumor that he had an almost 40-year affair with one of his slaves, Sally Hemings, and secretly fathered her six kids. We do know that Hemings went with Jefferson to France as a maid in 1787 at age 14 and came back two years later pregnant, but Jefferson never took credit for that pregnancy—or the five more to come. But, Hemings' children, and their descendants, have always claimed they're part of the Jefferson family tree. Jefferson's legitimate kids and their descendants, however, have always denied a second family.

THE PLAYERS

→ Thomas Jefferson
Founding Father

→ Sally Hemings
Jefferson's Slave and Rumored Mistress

→ Eugene Foster
Curious Scientist

In the late 1990s, curiosity finally got the best of Eugene Foster, a pathologist who lived near Monticello, Jefferson's 5,000-acre estate. Foster started looking into whether modern-day DNA testing could answer the question of Hemings' children's paternity. He conducted DNA tests, but even they weren't 100 percent conclusive. The best way to track ancestry is though the Y chromosome (which only men have), and Jefferson only had daughters with his wife, Martha. This meant that Foster had to use DNA from the male decedents of Field Jefferson, Thomas Jefferson's uncle, as well as DNA from one male decendant of Eston Hemings, Sally Heming's youngest son. The

Portrait of founding father Thomas Jefferson.

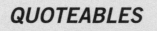

QUOTEABLES

"We hold these truths to be self-evident, that all men are created equal, that they are endowed by their Creator with certain unalienable Rights, that among these are Life, Liberty and the pursuit of Happiness."

Part of the Declaration of Independence, written by Thomas Jefferson, which seems in conflict with his slave ownership.

"Jefferson could date any eligible woman in the world. Why would he have an affair with a 15-year-old slave?"

John Works, an undisputed descendant of Thomas Jefferson, in an interview with *Time* magazine in 2004.

results proved that Eston was definitely a descendent of the Jefferson family, which suggested that Thomas Jefferson was *most likely* Eston's father. Despite the uncertainty, when Foster wrote up his findings in the journal *Nature*, the bombshell article was titled "Jefferson Fathered Slave's Last Child" making Foster's claim seem like a fact. Other magazines and newspapers reported on the article, but mostly left out the part about the tests not being 100 percent conclusive, spreading the belief the case was closed.

After the *Nature* article was published, the Thomas Jefferson Foundation (the nonprofit that runs Jefferson's Monticello estate) commissioned its own thorough research study to investigate the relationship between the former president and Hemings. Based on the study, the Thomas Jefferson Foundation concluded that Jefferson is the dad of Hemings' kid, and her story has been added to Jefferson's official history. However, the Monticello Association, which owns and maintains the official Jefferson family graveyard at the estate, is definitely not on the same page as the Thomas Jefferson Foundation. The Association is made up of more than 700 descendants of Jefferson and his wife Martha and, in 2002, it voted to deny membership to any of Hemings' descendants. Ultimately, they think all the evidence proves nothing and only makes Jefferson look bad.

THE AFTERMATH

The Rumor: The controversy over Jefferson's relationship with Hemings is ongoing. Many historians accept the Jefferson–Hemings relationship as historical fact based on the DNA evidence as well as historical evidence that proved that Jefferson was always at Monticello (where Hemings lived) when her children were conceived. The kids also supposedly looked remarkably like Jefferson, and were the only slaves he ever freed (two in 1822, and the rest in his will). Visitors to the Monticello estate, which is run by the Thomas Jefferson Foundation, will even learn about Hemings during the tour. However, many of Jefferson's undisputed descendants continue to deny any relationship with the Hemings family.

WHY WE STILL CARE

⭐ **The DNA testing of Jefferson's ancestors inspired other DNA tests.** Although Foster's DNA tests weren't 100 percent conclusive, they gave hope to people trying to track down their own ancestors. Since then, dozens of companies have popped up to provide inexpensive genetic testing. The tests have been especially important for African American families who, like Hemings' descendants, not only want to untangle family records that were poorly kept during the time of slavery but also want to learn more about their heritage.

⭐ **The scandal changes the way we view our founding fathers.** We often think of the founding fathers of our country as being upstanding men with strong morals. But to know that Jefferson probably took on a teenage slave mistress (and likely by coercion since she was so young and he literally owned her), impregnated her several times, and then denied the relationship until his death, shows us that the politicians who founded this nation were no more honest or moral than many today.

MORE US POLITICIANS WITH SECRETS

➡ **Franklin Roosevelt.** In 1921, former president Roosevelt was paralyzed from the waist down after contracting polio. He was in his early 40s at the time, and he managed to keep his paralysis a secret throughout his entire presidency. He rarely allowed himself to be photographed in his wheelchair and asked the press to keep quiet about it, which amazingly, they did.

➡ **Strom Thurmond.** The longest serving Senator in American history, Thurmond fought against civil rights for African Americans back in the '50s and '60s and even ran for president on a platform of racial segregation. That's why it surprised everyone when, six months after his death in 2003, African American Essie Mae Washington-Williams came forward claiming to be his illegitimate daughter. Thurmond's family admitted he knew about the daughter he fathered with his family's 15-year-old maid back in 1925, but left Washington-Williams nothing in his will.

➡ **Larry Craig.** In 2007, Idaho Senator Craig was nabbed in a police sting to catch men having sex in an airport bathroom. He pleaded guilty to disorderly conduct and resigned from the Senate over the scandal, but continuously denied being gay. In Congress, he voted against gay marriage, against expanding hate crimes laws to cover sexual orientation, and against making it illegal to discriminate against gay men and women in the workplace.

CUBA AND US IN CUSTODY BATTLE FOR FIVE-YEAR-OLD SHIPWRECK SURVIVOR

2000

THE SCOOP!

Five-year-old Cuban Elian Gonzalez found himself in the center of a highly publicized and politicized custody battle between the Cuban and American governments that took five months, tear gas, riot gear, and machine guns to end.

WHAT WENT DOWN

Cuba and the US are separated by only 90 miles of ocean, but the two countries aren't exactly friends. After Fidel Castro became Prime Minister of Cuba in 1959, he decided that Cuba should become a Communist country where the state owned all properties and ran all the companies. The US was (and still is) not too fond of Communism, so it cut off all ties and trade with Cuba. Cuba is a small island, and getting cut off hit them hard because they depended on US imports for almost everything. By the 1980s, their economy got so bad that thousands of Cubans fled their country via both legal and illegal means for nearby Miami, Florida. Before long, they created a strong anti-Castro exile community in Miami called "Little Havana."

THE PLAYERS

→ Elian Gonzalez
Five-Year-Old Cuban Shipwreck Survivor

→ Lazaro Gonzalez
Elian's American Great Uncle

→ Juan Miguel Gonzalez
Elian's Cuban Father

→ Janet Reno
American Attorney General

On Thanksgiving Day of 1999, a fisherman found five-year-old Elian Gonzalez floating alone in an inner tube off the coast of Florida. He and 12 other Cubans had fled their homeland earlier in the week on an overloaded aluminum boat that capsized and sank on its way to the US. Elian was one of only three survivors; his mom and step-dad were among the 10 who drowned. Usually, Cubans found trying to illegally enter the US are just returned to Cuba, but Elian and the other two survivors were allowed to stay pending an Immigration and Naturalization Service (INS) investigation. Elian's great uncle, Lazaro Gonzalez, lived in Little Havana and that's where Elian went to stay after he was rescued.

The story of this little boy who lost his mom while shipwrecked at sea was all over the news from the start, but it reached a new level of media attention when it came time to figure out what to do with him. To Cuban Americans in Little Havana, Elian was a symbol of freedom from Castro and Communism. They thought it would be cruel to send him back, especially since his mom died trying to bring him to the US. Anti-Castro politicians, mainly Republicans, also wanted to grant the kid US citizenship to show the US's distaste for the Communist regime.

But back in Cuba, Elian's dad, Juan-Miguel Gonzalez, who Elian had been living with before the shipwreck, said his ex-wife had taken off with his son in the middle of the night

Elian Gonzalez and his father upon their arrival in Cuba, 2000.

QUOTEABLES

"This was, in the end, about a little boy who lost his mother and has not seen his father in more than five months. The law has been upheld, and that was the right thing to do."

Democratic President Bill Clinton, defending Attorney General Reno's decision to take Elian by force on the day of the raid.

"A pre-dawn raid with tear gas and assault weapons on American soil to kidnap a 6-year-old is more reminiscent of Castro's communist Cuba than the America I thought I knew."

Republican Representative Tom Delay speaking out against President Clinton and Reno on the day of the raid.

without his permission. He wanted his son back home with him. Castro, who was still in power, also wanted Elian returned to his father but mainly because he didn't want the US to win this custody battle. He gave speech after speech demanding the kid be returned and pressed Cubans to go out to the streets and protest Elian's "kidnapping" by the Americans.

Ironically, the US federal government didn't have plans to keep Elian. The immigration department decided that Elian should be returned to his father in Cuba almost immediately. But Great Uncle Lazaro and the rest of the Miami family refused to hand the kid over and kept appealing to the courts for asylum and legal custody. Throughout the spring of 2000, there were marches, speeches, and protests in Cuba and Little Havana, each side claiming it only cared about what was best for Elian. The Justice Department tried to negotiate a peaceful handover of the boy, but Great Uncle Lazaro refused to budge.

As the frenzy grew, Americans—especially Attorney General Janet Reno—wanted to put the matter to rest. On April 23, 2000, Reno, who agreed with immigration that Elian should be returned to Cuba, gave the go-ahead for an early morning raid on Lazaro's house. A group of 20 federal agents wearing riot gear and armed with machine guns stormed in and grabbed the screaming boy at gunpoint. Elian was flown to Washington, DC, where he was reunited with his father, step-mother, and half brother.

THE AFTERMATH

The Raid: After the raid, hundreds of Cuban Americans protested in Little Havana, setting fires and throwing rocks at police. More than 200 people were arrested.

Elian Gonzalez: After Elian was reunited with his father in Washington, DC, they had to wait another two months for the Supreme Court to reject Great Uncle Lazaro's last petition for asylum. In June of 2000, Elian finally returned to Cuba and was welcomed home by a huge celebration. In 2008, Elian made headlines in both countries by joining the Young Communist's Union in Cuba.

Juan-Miguel Gonzalez: Elian's father still lives in Cuba and was elected to Cuban Parliament in 2003. He is often, along with Elian, a guest of honor at pro-Castro political rallies.

WHY WE STILL CARE

☆ **The battle over Elian had an impact on the 2000 Presidential election (page 206).** The election was held just months after Elian was returned to Cuba and ended up hinging on who won Florida's electoral votes. Many credit backlash from the Cuban community against Democrats (who had the Presidency and wanted Elian returned to his father) for pushing the Republican candidate George W. Bush ahead in the vote and into the White House.

☆ **The scandal influenced US relations with Cuba.** The custody battle brought a lot of attention to American–Cuban relations and made many Americans wonder why we were so hard on Cuba in the first place. Since the scandal, travel and trade restrictions between the US and Cuba have eased. In 2009, President Obama announced that Cuban Americans can make unlimited visits to Cuba and send money to family members who live there. The President also promised to make bigger changes to US–Cuba travel and trade restrictions.

MORE CUBAN-AMERICAN HISTORY

➡ **Spanish-American War.** At the end of the Spanish-American War in 1898, Cuba's colonizer, Spain, handed over control of the island to the US. In 1902, the US granted Cuba its independence but signed a treaty saying it could intervene to protect Cuba if needed.

➡ **The Cuban Missile Crisis.** In 1962, US spy planes photographed missile sites in Cuba being built by the Soviet Union—the US's biggest enemy at the time. Cuba's proximity to the US made this the worst possible news for then President Kennedy, who sent ships to block anything coming in or out of Cuba. For the next 12 days, the US and the Soviet Union were on the brink of all-out nuclear war until finally agreeing to a compromise that moved Soviet missiles out of Cuba and US missiles out of sites close to the Soviet border.

➡ **Guantanamo Bay Naval Base.** Though the US gave Cuba its independence in 1902, it kept a 45-square-mile area on the island for a naval base, which it held on to even after cutting off diplomatic and trade ties to Cuba. The base became famous after the September 11, 2001, attacks when President George W. Bush turned it into the main prison for suspected al-Qaeda members detained in the war in Afghanistan. Since then, the base has come under worldwide criticism, as suspects have been held there without trial and have been subjected to interrogation techniques many view as torture.

THE SCOOP!

In the closest Presidential race since 1876, Al Gore won the popular vote, George W. Bush won the electoral vote, and some votes were not even counted. It took 36 days, a controversial vote recount in Florida, and a Supreme Court decision to finally determine the next president.

WHAT WENT DOWN

The US voting system is complex. When you cast your ballot at the polls, you're really voting for your state's electors, and it's those people, collectively called the Electoral College, who actually elect the president. Each state has a specific number of electors depending on its population (for instance, California has 55 and North Dakota has 3), and each elector gets a vote. There are 538 electoral votes in all, so a candidate needs 270 or more to become the Commander in Chief. Most of the time, whichever candidate wins the most votes from the people (which is called the popular vote) also wins the electoral vote. But in 2000, that wasn't the case.

THE PLAYERS

➡ Al Gore
Democratic Nominee

➡ George W. Bush
Republican Nominee

➡ Katherine Harris
Florida's Attorney General

On November 7 of that year, Democratic candidate Al Gore won the popular vote against Republican George W. Bush (50.16 million to 49.82 million). But when it came time to count electoral votes, the numbers were too close to call an immediate winner. TV networks attempted to guess the outcome, and everyone had their eyes on Florida, the state whose 25 electoral votes could put either candidate over the 270 mark.

When the results finally came in for Florida, Bush was ahead, but only by 300 popular votes. It was a small enough margin to trigger a recount. Political lawyers and big shots from both parties flocked to Florida to try to control which votes would be counted—and how they'd be counted—so that their candidate would come out on top. Bush had a home-field advantage. His brother Jeb Bush was the governor, and the co-chair of George's Florida campaign, Katherine Harris, was Florida's secretary of state. The Florida Supreme Court originally gave Florida counties until November 26 to finish recounts, but a lot of counties weren't finished by then. Still, Harris went ahead and certified the electoral vote in Bush's favor (he had a 537 popular vote lead). Gore fought to get the decision overturned by

Gore supporters in Washington, DC, protesting for a fair recount.

QUOTEABLES

"Ignoring votes means ignoring democracy itself, and if we ignore the votes of thousands in Florida in this election how can you—or any American—have confidence that your vote will not be ignored in a future election?"

Al Gore, in a televised speech in November of 2000, urging Americans to be patient and continue Florida's recount.

"I am optimistic that we can change the tone of Washington, DC. I believe things happen for a reason, and I hope the long wait of the last five weeks will heighten a desire to move beyond the bitterness and partisanship of the recent past."

President George W. Bush's acceptance speech in December of 2000, during which he promised to bring the nation together.

the Florida Supreme Court so the counties could finish counting, but Bush went higher and appealed to the US Supreme Court to make the counting stop. What the Supreme Court says, goes, and on December 12 it voted five to four to uphold Harris' certified results and stop the recount.

Bush and his Republican supporters celebrated victory, but many saw the Supreme Court's decision as partisan. After all, it was the court's five most conservative judges who voted to stop the recount, which benefited Bush. Regardless, the battle was over. The final tally gave Bush 271 electoral votes to Gore's 266. The next day, Gore went on TV to concede, and Bush to promise to bring unity to a confused and divided nation.

WHY WE STILL CARE

☆ **The scandal forced people to reevaluate the Electoral College.** The Electoral College system has seemed both outdated and complicated for a while, but after the 2000 election, there was an especially strong motivation to change it. Since then, six states—New Jersey, Maryland, Massachusetts, Illinois, Washington, Vermont, and the District of Columbia—have passed legislation that will automatically give all the state's electoral votes to the candidate who wins the national popular vote, even if it's not the candidate who won in that state. But it won't go into effect until

THE AFTERMATH

George W. Bush: Though he promised to unify the country, many argue that Bush (just like his Democratic predecessor Bill Clinton) succeeded in dividing it along party lines. Perhaps his most divisive decision was the invasion of Iraq in 2003. Despite his critics, Bush was reelected for a second presidential term, winning against Democratic candidate John Kerry in 2004.

Al Gore: Everyone expected a Bush vs. Gore rematch in 2004, but instead Gore became more involved in a battle to save the environment. In 2006, he starred in a documentary about the effects of global warming called *An Inconvenient Truth*, which won two Oscars. In 2007, Gore won the Nobel Peace Prize for his work bringing worldwide attention to climate change.

other states holding a total of at least 270 total electoral votes adopt similar laws.

☆ **The scandal reminded Americans that their vote matters.** Less than half of eligible voters even bothered to come out for the 2000 presidential election. The closeness of the final vote, along with later accusations of voting fraud, reminded citizens that they do have a voice in politics. In the 2004 election, 6.4 percent more Americans took to the polls to decide who would be the next president. It was the biggest increase in voter turnout since the 1950s.

MORE TIMES MAJORITY DIDN'T RULE

➡ **1824.** There were four main competitors running for office: Andrew Jackson had the most popular votes and the most electoral votes, but not the 270 needed to win. John Quincy Adams, son of former President John Adams, was pretty close behind. Since no one won outright, the decision went to the House of Representatives. Representative Henry Clay, who had come in fourth in the popular vote, put his weight behind second-place Adams, convincing the House to choose him over Jackson. When Adams became president, he made Clay his secretary of state, a deal that became known as the "corrupt bargain."

➡ **1876.** New York's Democratic Governor, Samuel Tilden, won the popular vote by 300,000. But the electoral votes that would have gone to Tilden in three southern states (which were still under military occupation after the Civil War) were disqualified by local, Republican-run electoral boards. This meant Tilden's rival, Republican Rutherford B. Hayes, was still in the game. For the next few months, the House and the Senate argued over who would choose the president. It wasn't until January of 1877 that an Electoral Commission (comprised mainly of Republicans) decided that Hayes should get all the disputed votes, putting him ahead 185–184 and making him our 19th president.

➡ **1888.** Running for a second term in office, President Grover Cleveland won the popular vote, but got destroyed in the Electoral College vote, 233–168, by Republican Benjamin Harrison. The election was famous for voting fraud on both sides, but even without the majority of the vote, Harrison slid into office based on the electoral count without the kind of fight we had in 2000. Well, until four years later when Harrison ran against Cleveland again, this time losing both the popular and the electoral vote.

INDEX

➡ **A**

abortion, 45
Abrahamian, Ara, 21
abuse
    domestic, 82–85, 121, 189
    gay panic defense, 129
    police brutality, 166–169
    rape, 10–13, 34–37, 117,
        118–121, 143
    terrorist, 116
accident, death by, 98–101
acid (drug), 90, 92, 93
ACLU (American Civil Liberties
    Union), 42–45
activism. See political activism
Adams, Elizabeth "Madam
    Alex," 178–181
Adams, John Quincy, 209
affairs, 75, 100, 143, 189,
    198–201
African Americans
    Jefferson's slave affair, 198–
        201
    LA race riots, 168–169
    Miss America, 134–137
    OJ Simpson murder case,
        186–189
    Olympics civil rights protest,
        94–96
    police brutality, 166–169
    racial discrimination, 94–96,
        106–109, 138–
        141, 166–169,
        186–189
    slaves, 113, 198–201

Subway Vigilante shooting
    of, 138–141
unethical medical research
    on, 106–109
Aguilera, Christina, 161
AIDS medical research, unethical,
    109
alien invasion, 58–61
Allen, Barry, 138
Allen, Woody, 57
All the President's Men
    (Woodward &
    Bernstein), 112
Alpert, Richard, 90–93
Amateur Athletic Union, 20
Ambien, 129
Ames, Aldrich, 69
anarchy, 46–49, 177. See also
    protests; riots
ancestry, 198–201
animal rights, 17
Appeal to Reason, 14
Applewhite, Marshall, 125
April Fool's Day, 61
Arbuckle, Roscoe "Fatty," 34–37
Arista Records, 156
Arnaz, Dezi, 75, 89
Arnold, Ervin, 22–24
art controversy, 150–153
Asinof, Eliot, 29
assassination
    anarchist, 49
    character, 173
    gay rights activist, 126–129
    Kennedy, John F., 101, 141
    Reagan, Ronald, 13

ATF (Alcohol, Tobacco and
    Firearms, Bureau of),
    174–175, 176
athletes, Olympic, 18–21, 94–97,
    182–185. See also
    sports

➡ **B**

Bad Boy Records, 190
Baez, Joan, 105
Bailey, F. Lee, 116, 117
Bakker, Jim, 142–145
Bakley, Bonnie Lee, 37
Baldwin, Alec, 189
Ball, Lucile, 75
bank robbery, 115–116
Barrie, Dennis, 152
Barrows, Sydney Biddle, 181
Barry, Joan, 62–65
Barry, Marion, 131
baseball, 20, 26–29, 146–149
Bashir, Martin, 171, 172
Basinger, Kim, 189
Battle of Lexington, 177
Beaulieu, Priscilla, 72
beauty pageant scandals, 134–
    137
Be Here Now (Ram Dass), 92
Bell, Sean, 169
Bernstein, Carl, 110, 112
Beulah, 89
Biggie Smalls, 190–193
blackmail, 170–171
Black Panthers, 95
Black Sox, 26–29
Blades of Glory, 184
Blair, Katie, 137

ABOUT THE AUTHOR

Hallie Fryd is a writer living in Oakland, California. She studied history at Carnegie Mellen University and writes about politics and pop culture for her blog Psyched and Such (psychedandsuch.blogspot.com). She can't help but see connections between current events and stuff that happened 100 years ago, and hopes that, with *Scandalous!*, she's achieved her life-long dream to write a non-boring book about history.

ACKNOWLEDGMENTS

I'd like to thank Jake, Pam, Maria, Karen, and the internet without whom there would be no *Scandalous!*.

MORE POP CULTURE FROM ZEST BOOKS!

REEL CULTURE
50 Classic Movies You Should Know About
(So You Can Impress Your Friends)
by Mimi O'Connor

THE END
50 Apocalyptic Visions From Pop Culture You Should
Know About...before it's too late
by Laura Barcella

HOW TO FIGHT, LIE, AND CRY YOUR WAY TO
POPULARITY (AND A PROM DATE)
Life Lessons from 50 Teen Movies
by Nikki Roddy

OFF THE BUS AND ON THE RECORD
22 Candid Interviews by the Teen Journalists of
The Rock Star Stories
by Amanda, Brittany, Jaime, and Zac Rich
with rock journalist Aaron Burgess

In high school, Hollywood, and even the White House, rumors tend to trail after the biggest personalities (because hey, we've all got our secrets), but when a rumor becomes a full-blown scandal, well, the bigger they come the harder they fall. Richard Nixon, Roman Polanski, O.J. Simpson, and Milli Vanilli have all had some very hard falls—but they've also challenged us and made us change our expectations. If you think about it that way, scandals are a key part of American life. Maybe Madonna's bra and Elvis's hips should get their own Mt. Rushmore? Until then, we've got *Scandalous!*

GET THE SCOOP!

- Learn exactly what happened during the scandal, and who the key players were
- Hear unbelievable quotes from the people involved
- See how the event affected American culture and politics
- And follow the scandal's footsteps through a short list of related events (so you can see how, sometimes, history is doomed to repeat itself!)

This essential guide also includes a great photo for each of the 50 political and entertainment-related scandals. So after you've read *Scandalous!*, you'll have a better understanding of how Timothy Leary, Marilyn Monroe, and Michael Jackson (not to mention Bill Clinton and O.J. Simpson) helped to shape the world as we know it. And you may even become a history buff while you're at it.

US $13.99 (Higher in Canada)
ISBN: 978-0-9827322-0-5
1475813

51399

9 780982 732205

www.zestbooks.net